I Want 2 be Tendulkar!

I Want 2 be Tendulkar!

Manish Sharma

GenNext Publication

ISBN: 978-93-5324-103-2

Price : ₹ 199

First Published, 2016

Published by

GenNext Publications
5, Ansari Road
Daryaganj, New Delhi-110002
Phone: 9811692060
E-mail: gennext@hotmail.com

Printed at: G. Print Process, Delhi.

Cataloging in Publication Data—DK
Courtesy: D.K. Agencies (P) Ltd. <docinfo@dkagencies.com>

Sharma, Manish, 1979- **author.**
I want 2 be Tendulkar! / Manish Sharma.
pages cm
Novel.
ISBN: 978-93-5324-103-2

1. Cricket stories. 2. Indic fiction (English) I. Title. II. Title: I want to be Tendulkar!.

PR9499.4.S53I93 2016 DDC 823.92 23

Contents

In loving memory
Of my late mother
Vijay Sharma

Author Note

In life, more often than not, we keep searching to 'others' rather than exploring, or finding the proper ways to groom ourselves!! I have seen this at number of times. I am in 14th year of my journalism career, but this issue was striking in my mind for a too long. First, It surprised me long back when I found absolutely 'new & eye opener atmosphere' in U.P. Sports College, Lucknow, which has produced Test cricketer Suresh Raina and R.P. Singh as well. What I saw over there that a senior used to do worship of known legend cricketer of his time on daily basis and had stuck his poster in his wardrobe along with the Indian God. In my cricket journey, I saw countless parents making request to coaches that 'please somehow to make their son Tendulkar and they would pay to any amount for it'!! Really, it was too ridiculous and strange, but this was entirely true, a thought and state of mind which can't be overlooked. Or, could it be?

I saw that even few mature guys were too addicted with such 'mind' as there was a bowler used to spend almost at least two to three hours in net to match his action just like a legend bowler of his time. Surely, he was searching someone else in himself rather than exploring, or grooming himself, No. Was he not killing 'himself', his own characteristics and range?

By the way, matter went beyond the sportsas well once I visited National School of Drama (NSD) and saw number of promising actors and actresses were 'searching', or copying to 'others' during the rehearsal and they were almost frantic about their idols. The years later, I found such thing in newsroom in Television channels as well when almost every young journo was imitating the voice and style of known journalists/anchor rather than working on his/her plus minus. Surely, I have seen countless such people in every field and area.

Intimation and inspiration are two separate bank of any river. Everyone has been born with his or her own virtues and there is process to make it big, groom, or establish your own image and personality. Once you try to be like someone, you absolutely kill your virtues and your characteristics you are born with. One thing is very clear that it is not easy to realise your talent in early age, and one of toughest thing is to groom yourself the exact way anyone must be done! It's constant process or journey and it applies on all profession and each and every process has its 'own definition and walk and talk'.

I really have wanted to write and say about it, but was searching a solid story through which I could present the picture in very interesting and entertaining manner. In my cricket and journalism career, I have met various personalities, but it took too long for me to decide whom should I go ahead with. Finally, having given too much thought to the subject and to give the message, I choose 13 years old Nitin Srivastava of Kanpur. It took almost three years in research and giving final shape to this story. I have kept even minutest thing in my mind while penning it down, and of course, your entertainment as well. It was not easy at all while spending almost 12-13 hours in newsroom as it takes lot of toll, but I have tried my best to justify with the story. How justify I have done, it would be decided entirely by you?

In the last but not the least, I also would like to take this opportunity to dedicate my this dream book to my parents, wife, sister, nephew (Krishna, Arjun), brother-in-law, all relatives, all friends, my all Gurus (cricket coaches, journalism mentor and class teachers), fellow journalists, cricket fans, and yes to the one of the greatest batsman of the world, and India's proud **Sachin Tendulkar and all his fans.** I hope you all will read this book and your honest feedback.

Thank you very much

Manish Sharma

ONE

10:30 a.m.

There is a surge of media persons outside Kanpur Medical Centre. The condition is different as compared to last five days. As of today, a group of ten to fifteen journalists are converted into a huge crowd. Almost fifty journalists (there are more than eighty TV scribes), in groups, are engaged in discussing while others are setting their equipments. The noise made by them, is far more than the level of noise heard in any Indian vegetable market. The face of all the scribes are gripped in strange tension. Everyone is a centre of attraction for the people who are passing by on the road but contrary to this, the thirsty eyes of scribes, in regular intervals, are following each and every car that seems to be coming towards them.

The scenario is clearly giving a message that the people from media are desperately waiting for someone special. Suddenly a loud voice cut through the buzz of the noise. We have confirmed from our reliable sources that Nitin Srivastava's condition has improved a lot. It wouldn't be an exaggeration to say that today is the biggest day in Nitin's life. Finally, he would get the precious thing that he was asking for last five days and dreamt ever since he was a child. We will observe each and every moment and give you details of every single minute for the entire day. "Shilpi Saxena, with cameraman, Mohammad Shahid, from Kanpur, Aaj Tak."

As one of the most stunning and charming female anchors/ reporters of a leading news channel of India finished her p.2.c (piece to camera) and gave too much stress on last few words, a reporter from another channel gave a light pat on her shoulder from behind and said, 'Amazing! Shilpi, you are doing great. What a fantastic p.2.c you gave!'

'Hey *Saale** Was that a praise or mockery?' Shilpi stared at the Zee News reporter, Jitendra Kala.

'How can I make mockery of you? After all, you are the star reporter of India's number one news channel,' replied Jitendra.

'Stop buttering *Saale*. I know you gave your report much earlier than me.'

'How do you know?' Jitendra asked feeling embarrassed.

'Hey *Saale*, bamboo was fixed on my ass ever since your p.2.c was aired,' said Shilpi. As Shilpi replied in a loud voice, a fourteen year old boy looked at her, sporting a strange feeling on his face. Perhaps, that was the first time he heard a beautiful girl talking like boys.

'What do you mean?' Jitendra asked without noticing the boy.

'Hey, *Saale*, there was a flood of calls on my mobile ever since your p.2.c was aired early this morning,' Shilpi said sneering at him.

Jitendra burst into laughter.

'Hey, *Chootiye***! Why are you laughing like a eunuch?' the fourteen year old boy's eyes widened even more. In between, Jitendra's seyes collided with the boy's gaze while he was laughing.

'Come on' have some shame, atleast in front of the child. What will he think?' Jitendra was absolutely serious this time.

'Hey, *Chootiye!* This young generation is not less than our father these days. He is your father in terms of illegitimacy. Am I saying anything wrong?' she asked the boy. The boy ran away as soon as Shilpi threw a question at him. Saying this, she rolled out the cigarette's puff.

Jitendra burst into laughter once again.

'You are laughing like a eunuch again.'

'Why are you getting angry at me?' Jitendra asked being a little flared.

'*Saale!* Why didn't you wake me up early in the morning?' Shilpi looked at him angrily.

'Wooooo,' Jitendra's words were stuck in his throat.

---

*, ** Slang Word in India.

'What woooo! You came to Kanpur from Delhi with me. You stayed with me in the same hotel to save money but when it was the point of going to the hospital, you ditched me. Right?'

'Sorry dear, I forgot in a hurry.' Jitendra's face clearly expressed that he was lying.

'I know why you forgot. I have been in this bussiness for more than a decade,' Shilpi replied with another puff of his cigarette.

Jitendra laughed again.

If you make this laughing noise again, I will put the cigarette in your….' Shilpi tried to touch the cigarette on his back.

'Hey what are you doing? This is my new trouser.' Jitendra got up immediately and looked at his back.

'Don't be afraid, foolish man. I know you have purchased new trouser after almost a year,' she threw her cigrette, after taking the final puff.

'It's OK. Is there anything new going on in your life?' asked Jitendra.

'Nothing, really, as of now. Nitin Srivastava has overpowered my thinking.' Shilpi replied.

'You are absolutely right. It has been almost a week that because of him we can't eat and sleep properly.' Jitendra yawned.

'By the way when is "God" coming?' Jitendra blinked and inspected his wrist-watch.

'I am not a *Chootiya* like you. Just wait and watch,' Shilpi replied in a proud and confident voice. Her body language clearly showed that she knew the minutest detail of "God". So much so, that she would be aware of the colour of the under wear that "God". Though, every second journalist, whoever was present over there, was prone to being "diseased" of having deep news related to "God". However, Shilpi was different. She had that "X" factor in her. Time and again she had proved that and made her channel proud.

'How long the "God" will keep us waiting?' No sooner did he say that the noise became even more intense and all the T.V. scribes rushed towards a black Mercedes.

Even before the Mercedes stopped, it was surrounded by over fifty journalists at the gate of Kanpur Medical Centre. As soon as the dazzling car was stopped, a short man, wearing white track suit and black glasses stepped out. Around fifty questions echoed in different voices at the same time. The scenario was such that there was a competition amongst all the T.V. journalists to take their mike closer to the "God's" mouth.

Jatin Sir, 'What do you have to say about Nitin?'

'What will you say to Nitin?'

'What gifts have you come with?'

'Will you give any financial help to Nitin?'

Yes, he was none other than the legendry Indian cricketer, Jatin Tendulkar. As many mouths were there, those many questions were repeated again and again. Jatin was completely unfazed by the questions and simply ducked them, the way he does in the field against the best bowler of the planet.

'I will give all the answers but only after meeting Nitin. Thank you very much.' having said that, Jatin went back again in to his Mercedes. Soon, the car vanished through the gate of the hospital with two other vehicles. One was of his personal security staff and the other was a local police jeep that followed him right from the Landmark Hotel where he was staying in.

'*Namaskar* (Hello) sir, how are you?' A lady aged fifty plus got up immediately from a bench and rushed towards Jatin to greet him. An another lady got up and dragged a chair to offer to the master-blaster.

'*Namaste, namaste* (Hello). Please don't do that. I will take care of that,' Jatin said in a loud voice as he saw the young lady dragging a chair for him.

'By the way, how is Nitin?' Jatin pointed out towards the bed. The bed was laid on the left side of him at a distance of almost five feet.

'He is better now and capable of speaking,' the middle aged lady replied.

'Good, I was enquiring about him regularly ever since he got admitted. I decided to come here when I was assured that he is in a better state of mind to speak.'

'By the way, are you Nitin's mother?' Jatin said, who was yet to be seated in the chair.

'Yes sir, please sit down first. We are feeling embarrassed,' with both her hands folded the middle aged lady requested as she was still in a posture to greet Jatin.

'OK.' Jatin sat on the chair finally. He signalled his manager to sit as well, while the security person, along with the local policemen, was instructed to go out of the room by Jatin's manager.

'What's your name, aunty?' Jatin asked the middle aged woman after a silence of almost two minutes.

'Sir, I am Savitri Srivastava and, she is my elder daughter Reena.'

'Where is Nitin's father?'

'Sir, he is still on the bed and can't move,' Reena intervened.

'Oh! I am sorry, I forgot. Someone had told me about him.'

'Have you told Nitin that I would be coming to meet him?'

'Yes, but we didn't inform that you will come today.'

'OK.'

'Can I talk to him?' Jatin asked.

'No problem, sir. He is sleeping for almost three hours now,' Reena got off the bench to wake her brother.

'Hey Nitin, open your eyes. Hey, look who has come to meet you,' Reena shook Nitin's body softly, as he lay down, by turning his face towards the wall.

'Get up my brother, get up. How long will you sleep like this?' Reena shook him with more power this time.

'Come on *di* (sister). Please don't disturb me and leave me alone,' Nitin replied without opening his eyes and turned his face.

'Look my son, some one special has come to meet you.'

'Oh my God!' Nitin's mouth kept remain open wide as he turned his face towards his right side. He got up immediately and sat on the bed. He was absolutely stunned and speechless as he was yet to believe that the person whom he worshipped like God, right from his childhood, was actually in front of him. For almost two to three minutes, he looked at Jatin, his mother and then, towards his sister with surprised eyes. Suddenly he started weeping like a child.

'Hey don't cry Nitin...please don't.' Jatin tried to stand off the chair but Nitin's mother stopped him.

'Let him cry, sir. These are the tears of joy.'

Jatin sat again.

'Sir I was desperately.....'

'You don't need to come off the bed,' Jatin left the chair again and stopped Nitin as he saw that he was trying to get down. Jatin went close to him and dragged his chair as well. As Jatin came close to Nitin's bed, he hugged him while sitting on the bed and started weeping loudly again.

'No Nitin, don't cry. You are a brave boy,' Jatin rubbed his hand on his head. Nitin kept sobbing for the next five minutes and Jatin kept standing next to him, rubbing his head to console him. Once the sobbing was stopped, Jatin sat on his chair.

'Are you OK?' Jatin looked at Nitin with a broad smile.

'Yes sir, Getting a hug from you is the finest medicine for me', Nitin said, wiping out his tears.

'Why did you do all this?' Jatin asked in a bit of anger.

'Sir,'

'What?'

'Sir, I have been absolutely hopeless.'

'But, you were selected in India under-nineteen team.'

'Yes, sir but my destiny turned me down completely,' Nitin said.

'Nitin, I have heard that you worship me.'

'Yes, sir.'

'Your story seems to be very interesting, Nitin.'

'You can say sir, but the destiny ditched me again and again.'

'I want to listen to the story right from the horse's mouth.'

'It will take time sir, You might get late.'

'Will it complete in two hours?' Jatin asked staring at his wrist watch.

'In less than two hours.'

'Then, go ahead,' Jatin said.

Nitin started to narrate.

TWO

Almost six years back.

Kaushal Puri, Kanpur, 22nd April, 1998

'Come on, Jatin'...'Well done, Jatin'...'Keep it up, Jatin'... 'What a fantastic shot'...'Now India will surely win this match.' All these words were echoing in the small room around 10:30 p.m. The room was filled with twelve to fifteen guys and, all were supporting Jatin sitting in front of the television set. Some were sitting on an old single bed which made a grinding sound at regular intervals when almost six people jumped at each and every boundary. It gave tension to Seetaram. 'Don't be mad. My bed will break. I purchased this old one with my savings of two thousand rupees.' Seetaram's heart almost came out with every shot of Jatin.

'Don't worry, uncle. We will not break it. Just enjoy Jatin's batting,' the sixteen year old nephew of Seetaram replied.

'This cricket has destroyed everything. Jatin has made every second guy mad,' Seetaram yelled loudly in irritation.

'Come on uncle, please don't disturb us,' requested the nephew.

'Hey! What are you doing here? Go inside,' Seetaram shouted as he saw his thirteen year old son, Nitin, who was watching Jatin's batting closely holding the seventh class book in his hand. Nitin was completely lost in the match when Seetaram shouted at him once again. 'Are you listening or shall I give you a slap on your face?' This time the voice was almost three times louder than before. It worked. Nitin went inside his room.

'I will break your legs if you come out. You have an English exam tomorrow. Study properly.'

'Stop now, you have scolded him a lot. Don't shout like a mad man. Let children enjoy the game.'

'Well shot aunt! Well shot!' Seetaram's nephew, Ankit, turned his right side and smiled. Seetaram couldn't do anything except glancing him. He sat near the gate so that he could keep an eye on Nitin. The gate was the only link between the inner room and the room outside.

Nitin lay on the bed with both hands folded under his head and an unfolded book resting on his face. Whenever he realised that someone was coming, he started to read the book like a very hard working student but English exam was miles away from his mind and only the match was going on. Live commentary and Jatin's flood of shots had put Nitin at a complete unrest. Something started to cook in his mind and after almost five minutes, the thirteen year old Nitin proceeded with his strategy. He got off the bed and came to the door.

'How dare you come here?' Seetaram scolded Nitin and blocked the door with his leg.

Nitin put up his index finger as if he was in front of his school teacher.

Action spoke louder than words.

'Go and come back within five minutes,' Seetaram made way for him. He moved his leg away which was positioned in front of Nitin's stomach but even before five minutes passed, Nitin came back, stood near the old bed and started watching the match again.

'You will not stop, no?'

'*Papa*, I want to see Jatin's batting.'

'Jatin will not come to help you in your exam.'

'Let him see, *papa*. It's a matter of only half an hour as India is on the brink of victory,' Nitin's nineteen year old, only sister came in his support.

'You shut your mouth and mind your own business.'

Reena didn't resist after seeing the anger of her father.

'No, *papa*, I will see the match,' Nitin pleaded.

'Shut up and just go to your room,' Seetaram caught his hand and tried to push him into the room.

'No, I will see Jatin's batting.' Nitin tried his best to take his hand off but, soon, surrendered as he got a heavy punch by Seetaram on his back. He rushed inside weeping. As he entered the room, Seetaram locked the door from outside.

Seetaram's move removed Nitin's pain completely within seconds as everything was going on according to Nitin's plan. After almost five minutes, Nitin, too, locked the door from inside in slow-motion, so that no one could hear even the slightest sound. As the gate was locked, he started to execute his plan further. He picked up a small briefcase and put that on top of a big box. He, then, took a stool of two feet height and kept it on the briefcase by giving it support of the wall. In three attempts, he was standing on top of that stool. He took support of the loft which was almost twelve feet above the ground. Soon, he climbed onto the loft and found himself close to the small pipe fitted window, which opened to the other side towards the back room of the neighbour's house. As he peeped through the corner of the window, his face was lit up with a broad smile. He clenched his fists with joy. The neighbour's family members were too enjoying the cricket match.

Now Nitin could see the television clearly. He kept watching the match for next half an hour, until India won the match. When the match got over, he hardly took five minutes to put the briefcase and stool in the same order as they were just half an hour back. Having unlocked the door again in slow-motion, he laydown on his bed and the book was once again resting on his face. Soon, Seetaram entered the room.

'You are studying like this,' yelled Seetaram.

'Actually, *papa*, I caught up with my sleep just five minutes back.'

'It's OK. Keep studying and don't sleep before midnight.' Seetaram came out of the room and locked the door again from outside. Inside, Nitin was dancing with joy as he had made his way to watch another big encounter between India and Australia which was to take place in two days.

THREE

24th April, 1998

On this day, the story on Sharjah cricket ground was almost similar. The only difference was that just a day before, India had chased 285 runs successfully and now today, the Indian team was chasing 273 runs. But, in these two days, the only thing that did not change was Jatin's style of batting which put hammer on the Kangaroos. Yet another thing that remained unchanged was, the scenario Seetaram's small house. On the big day, at almost the same time, the room was buzzing with one sound.

'Come on Jatin! Come on…Well done Jatin! Well done! This time your hard work will not go in vain.' There were many more voices in the small room as compared to the last match. It was the impact of the wonderful century that Jatin made just a day before. There was a lot of encouragement for Jatin but nothing for Nitin's father Seetaram. He was preparing for his math's exam but when Jatin came to bat, he couldn't control himself and came out of the room in the hope that, perhaps, this time he would be allowed to watch his hero Jatin batting but only to listen to the same "dialogues" what he had heard the last day.

'Hey what are you doing here? You have been going bonkers because of the match. Just go inside and don't dare come out,' Seetaram scolded him and locked the door from outside. Nitin got exactly what he wanted. He followed the same plan that made him happy a day before. He enjoyed Jatin's another classic century through his window by sitting on the loft.

Fifteen days later.

4:25 a.m.

'Someone is beating the door,' Savitri said while lying on the bed.

'Who could it be so early in the morning?' Seetaram replied in his sleep.

'It seems to be a drunkard beating the door,' Savitri said.

'Yes, you are right,' Seetaram said after five minutes, when the knocking stopped.

'Oh God! These drunkards can't keep peace even so early in the morning.'

'Why are you taking pain? Sleep properly.' Saying this, there was no further conversation from either side but the knocking at the door was successful as Nitin came into an absolutely alert mode. He took his face out from the sheet and got off the bed so carefully that not even a single sound was created. He picked up his footwear from under the couch, held it in his hand and came out of the room. He entered the kitchen and took keys of the main gate from the sugar box. Soon he unlocked the door from while looking back at regular intervals.

'Yes, the job is done,' Vishal, a nineteen year old boy smiled as Nitin came out of the house.

'Did you face any problem?' Vishal asked.

'No,' Nitin replied.

'It's almost 4:45 a.m. What about the door lock? If any thief enters the house then what will happen?' Vishal became serious.

'Don't worry. I have made special arrangements.' Nitin winked at Vishal.

'What special arrangement?' Vishal's eyes widened with curiosity.

'Just look at what I do.' Having said this, Nitin closed the door from outside but there was still a gap between the doors. The gap was good enough to take an elbow through it. He took his right elbow through the gap, locked the gate even from outside and put a metal lock as well.

'What an idea Nitin!' Vishal said surprisingly.

'Shhhhhh,' Nitin put his finger on his lips.

'The job is done. Where are Rinku, Harbola and Naseem?'

'I have knocked at their door as well. I had told the trio last night to assemble in front of your house. Hope they come soon.'

'It's OK, and what about Pradeep and Rahul *bhaiya*?'

'They will reach the Ramleela ground directly.'

'Hello! Good morning!' a voice from behind stopped their conversation.

'Very good morning, you came at the right time,' Vishal said as he looked back. Rinku, Naseem and Harbola came on their respective bicycles.

'Nitin, you have to sit on the back seat of Rinku's bicycle along with the pads. Naseem you have to fit all the three stumps at the back seat and I will take two bats and a ball with me.'

'Hey Harbola, you have to pick up Raju from mid way. Is everyone clear?' Vishal looked at everybody one by one. He got affirmation from all.

'Also, remember that none of the bicycles will be too far from each other. Just remain within a range of 5-10 meters from each other,' Vishal said.

'OK,' many voices echoed together.

'And yes, take care of Nitin.' He is the youngest amongst all and also, our star player.'

'OK,' the same voices echoed again. Having heard that, Nitin, who had shown his talent a number of times in the park that was right in front of his house, was smiling amongst his seventeen to eighteen year old friends. Soon, the four bicycles were heading towards the city's largest ground.

5:25 a.m.

Almost ten to fifteen bicycles entered the ground simultaneously. It was a large ground spread in acres; jam packed with almost three hundred boys.

'Oh shit! I guess we are late again. There is no space to play,' Vishal said after inspecting the ground.

'It always happens because of Raju and Deepak,' Vishal shouted, sitting on the bicycle and resting his one foot on the ground.

'It's no use of shouting at them. We should move in and try to seek opposition's team members. They may have occupied somespace,' the youngest Nitin intervened.

'Yes, and be quick. He is right.' As Vishal said this, all the bicycles started to move quickly.

'Look, Vishal, look. Rajesh and company are waiting over there,' Raju yelled from the back seat of the moving bicycle by pointing towards his left side as he saw the captain of the other team. The match was fixed for five hundred rupees, a leather ball and, of course, the pride of their locality was at stake.

'Hey, "glass boy" you really can see farther than us. Turn all bicycles towards the left side,' Vishal ordered and all the bicycles turned to left.

'Hey Rajesh! How are you? Congratulations! This time you have reached earlier than us.' Vishal stopped his bicycle and shook hands with Rajesh.

'Yeah but all in vain. The entire ground was already covered. We couldn't occupy any space,' Rajesh said.

'Oh shit!' Vishal said while hitting the handle with anger.

'Not a big problem. We will have to wait for five overs only. That match is about to get over,' Rajesh said, pointing towards a match that was at its peak.

'Have you told them to hand over the pitch to you?'

'Yes, I have spoken to them. Even then, inform your team members to be ready with the stumps, so that no other team could come and occupy,' Rajesh replied.

'I have given three stumps to each guy. Look after yours.' Rajesh gave a smile to Vishal.

'Naseem and Harbola, be ready with the stumps as the match is about to be over.' Both of them immediately came in to action as they listened. After almost twenty minutes, both teams' enthusiastic young members became busy with the preparation of their match.

'Fuck off', Vishal cried, hitting at the top of stumps with the handle of a bat.

'What happened Vishal?' Rajesh asked loudly who was busy along with his few mates, in the same process at a distance of about twenty two yards.

'It's very tough to fix stumps through the ground. You know that this ground is too hard,' Vishal said, hitting at the top of the stumps with a lot of power from the horizontal bat.

'Send someone to the temple. He will bring the water in polythene.'

'We don't have polythene.'

'Then don't waste time, Vishal. Apply the "old formula."'

'Yes, I have no other option,' Vishal said, hitting the stump with his feet. He was sweating badly.

'Make a hurdle please. Come, at least eight guys come, except Nitin and Raju,' Vishal the captain, said loudly by pointing towards his team members who were sitting at the dais, which was almost five hundred meter away from the pitch, where stumps were to be fixed. Soon, five members started running towards Vishal. After reaching there, they formed a circle and started to pee to make almost one foot area wet.

'How long will you pee Naseem?' Vishal said, having zipped up his trouser.

'How much will he pee? Hey *saale*, why do you drink so much water?' Rinku said. Naseem was still peeing while remaining five had finished their job.

'My job is done, too,' Naseem said while shaking his....

'Yes, it has been wet enough to fix all the three stumps,' Vishal said. All their brave efforts paid well and soon the stumps were fixed easily.

'Be quick, Vishal. Toss has to be done quickly,' Rajesh said, looking at his wrist watch.

'Yes friends, you all go and sit at the dais except the two of you. We are going for the toss,' Vishal said loudly and pointed towards two of his players to come with him. All of them followed him as not only he was one of the eldest among all but also, earned respect from opposition team.

'We will play a match of twenty overs. Twenty five is too much.'

'We have no problem,' Rajesh said.

'Do you have a coin?' Vishal asked.

'Yes, I have,' Rajesh immediately put his right hand into his pocket.

'What will you take, head or tail?' Rajesh showed the coin of one rupee.

'Look, this is head and this is tail,' Rajesh described by turning the coin.

'I know very well. We are not tossing for the first time,' Vishal replied.

'I will go for head, OK,' seeing closely three-four times, Rajesh tossed the coin up. All eyes followed the coin wing until it rested completely on the ground.

'Yes, we have won again,' Vishal raised his hands with fists clenched. He, along with two play mates stood up and made a sign of "V" towards the team members who were desperately waiting to know the result.

'We will be informing you about our decision within few minutes,' Vishal ran to discuss with his team mates.

'Not more than five minutes,' Rajesh said.

'Don't worry, dear.'

'We will bat first,' Vishal cried in even less than five minutes as he reached the dais.

'Nitin and Monty, put your pads on. Both of you will go for the opening,' Vishal instructed. Soon, both the openers were ready.

'Monty, keep Nitin's running in your mind. He is younger and slow as well,' Vishal was guiding his openers. On the other side, Rajesh was busy setting the field.

'It's OK,' Monty replied while practicing a drive without involving the ball.

'If he gets run out because of you Monty, I will break your legs,' Vishal said by showing him the stump.

'Nitin, we all are looking up to you. Just go and show your class.' Nitin just nodded to Vishal.

'Well done. Just go.' Both started walking to their respective ends. Nitin had to face the first ball.

'Vishal, send one of your players for umpiring too,' Rajesh shouted from the other point.

'Shikhar, just go for umpiring,' Vishal ordered.

'Well done Nitin....Well done Monty....Come on Deepak!' Soon, such names were echoing in the air again and again.

'Javed, please go back a few steps.' Deepak was the star bowler of Kidwai Nagar who was instructing the cover fielder. Seventeen year old Deepak started running with a brand new ball. He bowled the first delivery with full speed, but only to hide his eyes with the right hand. The ball was lost in the sun shine.

'Come on my Jatin, come on...Well done!' Vishal stoodoff the dais with joy. Same condition was of his remaining team members as well. Rajesh and his fielders were stunned to see that the thirteen year old Nitin had sent the very first ball over sixty yards.

'I am sure he will wash Rajesh's team off today,' Raju said. In between Deepak started to run again for the second delivery. He bowled even faster than the first ball, but this time he looked above his head. Once again, Nitin sent this over pitch delivery absolutely straight. It was a huge six over the long off and it cleared the distance almost sixty yards again.

'What a shot Nitin! Just like Tendulkar.' Vishal started clapping along with his play mates.

'Don't worry, everything will be fine. Keep it up guys, keep it up, well done Deepak, well done!' Rajesh was trying his best to keep the moral up for his star bowler but, Deepak's body language changed after the first two balls. In the next two deliveries, thirteen year old Nitin shattered the sixteen year older bowler's pride as the next two balls got the same treatment. One went over the extra cover and the fourth ball went over the deep square leg boundary again. Nitin's team mates were dancing and whistling at the dais.

'Nitin it's enough, be cool, be cool. Enough runs have come. Give the strike to Monty now,' Raju told Nitin coming close to him. Vishal sent Raju to give instructions to him with the batting gloves but captain's instruction didn't work at all. Till eleventh over, Nitin almost murdered every bowler. By the time he got run out, he had made 87 off 33 balls.

'Well played, my Tendulkar, well played. I am proud of you,' Vishal almost took Nitin into his lap and kissed on his cheek. Rajesh's team members were clapping and the applauding sound did not stop even on the dais for few minutes.

'Hey, can you provide any of your players?' Suddenly a voice compelled Vishal to look back.

'Yes, Bunty *bhai*,' Vishal stood up as he looked back.

'Brother, suddenly one of our players had to rush back home. We have almost lost the match as we require twelve runs in an over. Nine of our wickets are already down but we don't want to give one thousand rupees to opposition so easily,' said Bunty.

'OK, Nitin, go with Bunty *bhai*,' Vishal instructed Nitin who was yet to put his pads and gloves off.

'Why are you kidding me? Why are you sending a kid?' an eighteen year old Bunty made a mockery of Nitin as he saw him.

'Don't laugh Bunty *bhai*. He is our star batsman and has just scored 87 off 33 balls.'

'Really!' Bunty became serious.

'Come with me *Chhotu*,' Bunty caught his hand and took him.

'Ha-ha-ha-ha-ha,' the sound of many laughters burst at the same time. Almost twenty five boys were laughing upon seeing Nitin, as both, having crossed almost two hundred meters by running, reached the match place. Nitin's innocent face had no expression.

'Hey, you didn't find a younger player than him?' a voice echoed.

'Ha-ha-ha-ha-ha,' even louder sound echoed once again.

'Yes, he is the best option available as of now. And yes, *Chhotu*, you are going to bat,' Bunty said in an irritated voice.

'How many runs do you require to win?' Nitin asked with innocence.

'Ha-ha-ha-ha-ha,' Nitin went on to the ground casting a deep gaze on those eighteen to twenty one years old boys, who laughed at his question.

'*Bhaiya*, can you tell me how many balls are left and how many runs are required?' Nitin asked the umpire taking guard of the leg stump.

'Four balls are left and you need twelve runs to win,' the umpire replied.

'Surround him closely....go up to him,' the opposition's' captain shouted loudly. Soon, almost a twenty one year old bowler started running at lesser speed than normal and, as he bowled, all were completely stunned.'

Nitin sent the bowler back over the long off for a huge six.

'Come on *Chhotu*,' What a shot! Well done my tiger!' Such words and sound of clap were echoing in the air. All those boys, who were laughing at Nitin just a couple of minutes back, started dancing but captain of the opposition team kept encouraging the bowler till he reached his bowling mark. Everyone was keeping an eye on the next ball. Captain of the opposition team, who had set a close field for the previous delivery, sent the fielders on the boundary and came into a serious mode.

'Come on Vijay,', 'Come on,' 'That was just fluke,' 'We will surely win,' the captain was giving full back-up to his bowler along with his fielders. The bowler increased his run-up five steps more as compared to the last delivery. This time, Vijay ran faster than his normal speed. He took a high jump on the bowling crease and put all his strength behind the shoulder. It was a very sharp bouncer but even then this time, Nitin had hit the longest six of both of his innings he had played.

'Yes.... yes....... Hip-hip hurray!' All the boys ran towards the ground as if there was a competition to touch Nitin first. He started moving towards them with a cool state of mind as he was before when he went in to bat. Soon, Nitin was sitting on the shoulder of one of the boys. Someone was kissing him, others were congratulating him. This celebration, which was full of energy, went on for almost fifteen minutes.

'Take this, Nitin,' Bunty forwarded his right hand towards Nitin with two notes of hundred rupees each.

'No *bhaiya*, no,' Nitin tried to push Bunty's hand back.

'You deserve this. It's because of you that our team has won two thousand rupees today had we lost. It would have cost us the entire money. Saying this Bunty put two hundred rupees into Nitin's pocket and he too, didn't resist this time.

'Which school have you been to?' Bunty asked Nitin.

'Sardar Patel Inter College, *bhaiya.*'

'Hey, I am also in SP Inter College but I never ever saw you.'

'*Bhaiya,* I am in seventh class and there is a huge wall between sixth to ninth classes and twelveth.' .

'Yes, you are right. After fifteen days, I mean after summer vacations, we have fixed our match with Green Park hostel. It is a very important match. Be ready, you will definitely play that match. Being captain, I promise that you will play in eleven. I will convince our coach.'

'Thanks *bhaiya.*'

'OK, but keep coming here regularly so that you get enough practice.'

'Have you ever played on the matting wicket?'

'What is this *bhaiya* ?' Nitin asked with innocence.

'Hmmmm,' Bunty started contemplating.

'Don't worry. You just keep making runs here. I will make you play three to four matches in next fifteen days with us. I will take care of everything else.'

'Thanks, *bhaiya.*'

'Good Bye, *chhotu.*'

FOUR

Twenty days later......

'Nitin...Nitin...Where is Nitin?' Seetaram entered the house with a lot of anger.

'What happened? Why are you shouting?' Savitri came out in nervousness.

'Where is Nitin?' he asked as his eyes met Savitri's.

'Is he playing in the park?'

'Call him immediately otherwise I will beat and drag him to the house.' Seetaram's face was giving no less than the expression of Amitabh Bachchan of seventies.

'First tell me, what has he done?'

'Today, his class teacher met me on the way.'

'OK, so, what happened?'

'He has asked me to pick the report card, rather than Nitin taking it himself.'

'Why?'

'He didn't give me the details. Nitin has definitely failed.'

'Hmmmmm,' I will just call him. You sit inside and talk to him politely,' Savitri said.

After almost seven minutes, Nitin was standing in front of his father and sweating badly.

'Nitin, how were your exams?' Seetaram asked.

'All exams went off fine papa,' Nitin replied.

'Think twice before replying Nitin. Put pressure on your mind.'

'No papa. I did very well in all my exams.'

'Then why has your class teacher called me to take your result card?'

'I don't know,' Nitin said with innocence.

'Definitely, you would have done something wrong.'

'No, *papa*.'

'If you have done anything wrong, I will break your legs,' Seetaram scolded again.

'Why do you keep scolding him every time? Go outside and mind your own business. Savitri stared at her husband. Wife's loud words and anger worked. Soon, Seetaram left the house.

Next Day

'Stop here, brother,' Seetaram called the person who was driving the auto rickshaw.

'Move fast, we are running out of time,' Seetaram told Nitin. Both of them started to run on the wide road.

'Has the function started?' Seetaram asked the person as soon as he reached the gate of Sardar Patel Inter College.

'Yes, move inside the main hall.'

'O. K. thanks a lot.'

Within minutes, Seetaram entered the big hall, sporting nervousness on his face while catching Nitin's finger. The function was already on and the college principal was delivering his speech on stage. In front of the stage, almost fifty chairs were lying on both the sides. One row of chairs was on one side and the second was just in front of it. In between the rows of chairs, around five hundred children were sitting, some with tension on their face and others looking nervous. All the seats were occupied by teachers or other staff members of the school.

Seeing that no vacant seat was left, Seetaram chose the last corner of the right row to stand. Soon, voice of the person hosting the programme took everyone's attention and there was pin drop silence in the hall.

'I would like to take this opportunity to thank our principal for his fantastic and motivational speech. Now, I would like to call on stage, all the nine toppers of classes sixth, seventh and eight to collect their result card along with their prizes. Let us start with Amit Bansal from class eighth, who got top position in all three sections.'

As a young and good looking teacher-cum-host announced this, the entire hall echoed with the sound of clap. Soon, Seetaram's face was lit up as he saw that the boy returned to his front seat after taking the report card. He, then, touched his parent's feet. Upon seeing that, Seetaram got the idea that Nitin, too, has done something special, that's why he has been called to the function. Only a few seats of the first row were reserved for parents, and Seetaram knew them very well. But, soon the shine from his face vanished. Nitin's name was not called out by the host among the three toppers of class seventh. As the last boy of sixth class got his stuff, the host took over the stage once again.

'On behalf of all the teachers and principal of our school, I congratulate the boys and girls, along with their parents, who got the top position in their respective classes. By the way, the remaining students can get their report cards from their respective class teachers. All of you thank you very much.' As the announcer finished, people started leaving the hall. All students rushed to their respective classrooms, inviting a stampede in the hall.

'Where is your class room?' Seetaram asked in a reprimanding tone.

'We will have to go to the first floor.' Both of them reached the first floor.

'Sir, *Namaste,* 'Seetaram greeted the class teacher by folding both his hands.

'How are you Seetaram?' Around fifty years old man, Suresh Sharma, peeped through his glasses, chewing betel.

'Tell me, what's the matter?' Suresh asked spitting in the basket.

'Sir, actually you…,' Seetaram's words were stuck in his throat.

'Oh, yes. I forgot that I called you myself,' Suresh said, giving a light pat on his forehead.

'Seetaram, please give me ten minutes. Let me distribute the other cards, till then, you sit outside. I will call you soon,' Suresh said taking the bundle of result out of a box kept on the table.

'OK, sir.'

'Let Nitin sit here with his friends.'

'OK Suresh *ji.'* Seetaram came out of the room and sat on a chair.

'Yes, Seetaram, come in.' Seetaram was in the room within minutes as Suresh called him almost after fifteen minutes.

'Yes sir,' Seetaram folded his hands again.

'Nitin, you please sit outside for a while,' Suresh looked at Nitin.

'OK, sir.' Nitin left the room worried as he was yet to know his fate.

'Has Nitin cleared his exams, sir?' Seetaram asked with nervousness as Nitin went out.

'No need to be worried Seetaram. He has not only passed, but also got fifth position in his class.'

'Thank God!'Seetaram looked up at the roof with folded hands.

'Actually I had called you for a different reason,' Suresh said.

'Is there anything special?'

'Yes,' Suresh replied while placing a bundle of copies on the table. He took one copy out of the bundle and started turning its pages.

'Look at this,' Suresh turned the pages and tried to show the second last page of the exam copy.

'What is this, sir?'

'Please sit down and read it.' First time Suresh offered Seetaram chair but with reluctance.

'Sir, actually...,' As Seetaram saw the copy's second last page he looked at Suresh with surprise.

'Oh! Sorry, I forgot that a peon cannot read English.' The apology made was enough to humiliate Seetaram and make him realise his status in the society.

'You can do one thing. You take this copy along with you and return it to me within a week after photocopying the second last page. Once you read it, you will understand the matter easily.' Suresh finished the sentence after taking a pause of almost thirty seconds.

'OK, sir. Thanks a lot.' Seetaram folded his hands for the last time and left the room.

'What happened, *papa*?' Nitin got off the chair as he saw Seetaram and rushed to him to know his fate.

'You got fifth position in your class for first time Seetaram smiled with pride.

'Yes…yes,' Nitin threw his fists in the air as if he won the match, or celebrated any wicket. He ran and embraced his father.

'OK, it's enough. Move fast, your mother must be waiting.'

FIVE

'Yes, what happened?' Savitri came out running from the room inside as she heard the sound of footsteps.

'Mummy, I have stood fifth in my class,' Nitin ran and embraced his mother.

'My son!' Savitri hugged him and started kissing on his forehead and cheek.

'I knew my son would have done something special, that's why he was called with his father,' Savitri said.

'Yes, my brother is a hero,' Reena also came out.

'Yes, your lovable son and brother has done a very special thing as well, 'suddenly Seetaram got angry.

'Now, what happened? At least keep quiet today. Nitin has got fifth position in his class. Be happy,' Savitri said.

'Look, what he has done,' he shouted again while taking the exam copy out of his bag.

'What is this?'

'Just read the second last page.' Seetaram forgot in anger that it was no less than a blank sheet for Savitri also.

'How can I read this? It is written in English,' Savitri said, with surprise.

'Papa forgets everything in anger. He is the next angry young man after Amitabh Bachchan. Show it to me,' Reena snatched the copy from Savitri's hand and started reading.

'Hmmm,' Reena took a long breath after reading it. Both Savitri and Seetaram's faces sported curiosity.

'Come inside.' The trio followed her as if they were ordered by the boss.

'Why did you write all this?' Reena made Nitin stand between her legs. She caught both his hands and gave two slaps on Nitin's face. It left a red mark on his cheek.

'Yes, speak, why did you write all this?' Tears started rolling on Nitin's cheek.

'Sorry *didi.*'

'Tell us, we also want to know what he has written,' Savitri shouted.

'Then listen.' Reena started narrating the English essay about "Your father" in Hindi which was given to students to write in minimum 150 words. The subject could be any and Nitin chose to write about his father. His words were:

My father's name is Seetaram Srivastava. He works as a peon in a leading private school of Kanpur. He is very strict and choleric. More often than not, he keeps our family disturbed and tensed. My father always keeps scolding my mother, sister and me. More so, he hates my favourite sport, cricket, and my hero, Tendulkar. He doesn't allow me to watch cricket match on television, and keeps cursing cricket and Tendulkar most of the time. I have been asking for a bat for long, but he never brought it for me. After coming back from duty, he plays cards almost everyday, and fights with his friends as well. I wish that God gives him wisdom and generate love in him for cricket, Tedulkar and, allow me to watch cricket. I will pray to God that he scolds my sister and mother a little lesser.

Why did you write all this, tell?' Savitri shouted, and as she lifted her hand to slap, Reena caught her mother's hand.

'Leave it mom, he is a child and has already been punished. We actually need to think seriously why he wrote so?' Reena's logic converted Seetaram and Savitri's anger into seriousness.

SIX

The next day…

5:27 a.m.

As Nitin heard the knocking sound on his door, he quietly got down from the bed. Having picked up his shoes, he immediately walked towards the kitchen to take the keys of the gate. He searched all the boxes of tea, sugar and salt, but he did not find the keys of the door. After realising that his mother had repositioned the keys, he walked towards the main gate.

'What happened?' Vishal asked.

'It seems to me that mom has hidden the keys,' Nitin replied.

'Oh, what will happen now?' Vishal murmured while peeping through small space between the two gates.

'Let me think for a while,' Nitin said.

Be quick, Nitin. Match will start exactly at 7:00 a.m. It is already 5:40 a.m. and you know that it will take at least forty minutes to reach the Green Park stadium.

'It's OK. Have you brought shoes and the white dress?'

'Don't worry. I had arranged the stuff yesterday only.'

'Just check it out. Is *Lala's* shop open?'

'Yes, the gate is open,' Vishal replied after inspecting the shop. Actually, the wall of Nitin's house was a support for a heap of sand.

'Then, I will meet you after five minutes. You reach over there.' After saying that, Nitin headed upstairs and reached the roof of his house. He, then, climbed an almost five feet high wall and looked down. It was almost fifteen to twenty feet of distance between the ground and him but, the heap of sand was reducing it by almost ten feet.

'Jump properly, else, you will get hurt,' Vishal said, worried.

'Nothing will happen. I have done this so many times,' having said that, he jumped on the heap of sand. Nitin's legs were stuck half into the wet sand. Vishal supported him to come out of it.

'Be quick and take this bag. Your kit and dress are in this bag,' Vishal said while handing over a bag to Nitin. Vishal got ready with his bicycle. Nitin sat on the back seat, and soon the bicycle was talking with air!

'Hi Vishal, be quick,' Bunty said with excitement from almost a hundred meters as he saw Vishal coming to him.

'Have you brought the white dress for Nitin?' Bunty asked as Vishal stopped the bicycle in front of the main gate of the Green Park stadium.

'Yes, I had arranged for it yesterday only.'

'That's good. Park the bicycle in the corridor of the stadium. Nitin, you come with me.' As Nitin and Bunty reached inside the pavilion of Green Park, the other team members started to smile sarcastically, looking at Nitin. All, eighteen to twenty year old boys, were surprised to see a relatively younger player in the opposite team.

'Hey, why are you looking at him as if he were a portent, put on your kit quickly as the hostel team is about to reach.' As Bunty, the captain of S. P. Inter College, shouted on the team mates, they swung into action.

'Nitin, you too, put on your kit,' Bunty said.

'*Bhaiya*, can I wear the kit in the bathroom?'

'Ha-ha-ha-ha-ha,' suddenly a burst of laughter echoed in the big room.

'Why are you laughing on a child?' Bunty shouted again on the team mates while trying to control his own laughter.

'No problem, you can change your dress wherever you are comfortable,' Bunty said.

'Thanks *bhaiya.*'

'Hey Nitin, have you got supporter (cricketgear)?' Bunty asked as if he remembered something.

'No, *bhaiya.*'

'Hey Amit, give your supporter to Nitin as you are not going to play today,' Bunty pointed to one of his teammates. Soon, Nitin left the room with all the stuff to change his dress in the bathroom.

'Fuck off', Bunty shouted as S. P's fourth wicket fell down. The score board was showing only 38 runs off eleven overs. It was a match for forty overs.

'It seems that we will not be able to bat even for twenty overs. It was a good opportunity for our top order batsman to impress Khandekar sir but, everyone has let him down,' Bunty kept jabbering till the batsman entered the pavilion.

'Hey Pawan, stop. Nitin, you go and bat,' the captain's order changed the expressions on Pawan's face as he returned after walking ahead.

'Why are you sending him? He is a child.' Kanwal intervened with a lot of surprise.

'I have confidence in him. That's why I am sending him,' Bunty tried to pacify his vice-captain. 'But, Nitin was saying he never ever played on a matting wicket.'

'Let's see, what happens,' Bunty took a long breath.

'You go on Nitin, don't waste time,' Bunty instructed Nitin, who was listening to the conversation between the captain and vice-captain. 'Just play with straight bat, and no need to worry about the runs. There is no need to get intimidated with the speed and height of bowlers,' Bunty gave instructions to Nitin for the last time by putting his hand on Nitin's shoulder. As Nitin walked up to the pitch, the boys from the hostel, too, started looking towards him strangely.

'Why did you fix the match with S. P. College? It seems as if you have just come here to pass your time.' One of the hostel players looked towards his captain and said angrily.

'Concentrate on your job. Khandekar sir had set up this match, not me.'

'Just look at him, didn't they have a younger player than him,' remarked the player who was fielding.

'Take it sportingly. Come on boys, come on...be serious,' the captain boosted his players, but only to be surprised. As Uttar Pradesh's one of the best under-nineteen bowler bowled with a casual approach, Nitin sent it through the cover boundary for four. Nitin's fantastic cover drive compelled most of his team mates to come out of the pavilion in scorching heat. They stood outside the boundary line, sporting curiosity on their faces.

'Come on Shalabh...come on...'it was just a fluke'...'it happens in cricket,' the captain and fellow fielders tried to remove embarrassment from the bowler's face by speaking encouraging words, and clapping. That time, Shalabh took his full run-up. He ran down faster, and put more power through his shoulder. It was short of good length delivery, but once again, it met with the boundary line. The only difference was that this was a straight drive. Two consecutive boundaries had changed the body language of not only fielders, but his team mates as well. The head coach of Green Park, Deepak Khandekar, started to walk around the boundary to have close look of Nitin. Khandekar was rewarded as he got an opportunity to be the witness of the third consecutive four as the ball came to him straight through the point with a superb cut shot.

'Fine shot,' all fielders turned up to point towards the boundary. Words were echoed with the sound of clap by Deepak Khandekar but, by then, Shalabh's mood got jacked. His last ball was left to be bowled. Even that time, he ran a lot faster, perhaps knowing that he may be replaced by the captain, he put more power behind his shoulder. Suddenly, one voice echoed in the Green Park stadium.

'Bastard! Will you kill the child?' Shalabh's sharp bouncer compelled Deepak Khandekar to abuse him. Shalabh's bouncer hit Nitin's helmet, and his helmet fell down on the ground. Even his playmates didn't like it and most of the fielders, including the captain, Rakesh Yadav, ran up to him to have a word.

'Sorry *Chhotu,* sorry,' Shalabh ran up to the batting crease as he realised his mistake.

'I am OK, no problem,' Nitin's reply brought more embarrassment on his face. Bunty and his few mates ran inside the ground, but Nitin stopped them by giving a signal. After this, Nitin continued to bat till mid over, twenty four. During that period, many beautiful shots came from the "sweet part" of his bat. When Shalabh was brought back into attack again in the twenty second over, Nitin scored three consecutive boundaries. Before sacrificing his wicket for his senior pro, Nitin made 76 off 52 balls. In less than two hours those boys greeted him personally, who laughed at him.

'Well done boy...well played,' Deepak Khandekar gave heavy pat on his shoulder as he came almost five steps in, of the finishing line from the ground.

'Which team do you play for?'

'Sir, this was my first match at this level,' Nitin replied with innocence and he was sweating badly.

'Hmmmm,' Khandekar said, thinking seriously.

'Take Nitin, drink it.' In between Bunty offered him an energy drink. Putting off the helmet he drank it.

'Where do you live boy?' Suddenly a voice came from behind.

'Hey Tiwari *Ji*, when did you come?' Khandekar immediately walked to a forty five year old guy and greeted him by shaking hands.

'I came long before and was enjoying his batting from the left public stand,' Dharmendra Tiwari said. Tiwari was not only the chairman of the District Cricket Association but also one of the richest businessmen of Kanpur city. He had come to watch the performance of his fourteen year old son.

'Tiwari sir, you could have come to the pavilion.'

'Sir, you know that I always love to watch my son batting by hiding myself as I don't want to put any kind of pressure on him but, our hero got out cheaply even this time,' Tiwari's face lost shine.

'Don't worry Tiwari *Ji*. You must send Kapil daily to practice in Green Park. Everything will be OK,' Khandekar said.

'Yes, I will think about this. By the way as Kapil got out, I was about to leave the ground. But as that child took entry, he gained my attention and I decided to watch his batting,' Dharmendra Tiwari said while pointing out to Nitin.

'I am very lucky that I got a chance to see his batting. Really, I enjoyed it a lot. By the way, where do you live, Nitin?'

'Sir, I live in Kaushal Puri.'

'What! You live in the back side of my colony. I have never seen you.'

'Sir, this was Nitin's first match at this level. Can you believe that?' Khandekar's reply sewed Nitin's lips as he tried to open his mouth.

'Who brought you here?' Tiwari questioned with surprise.

'Sir, I brought him,' that time pride could easily be noticed on Bunty's face as he responded to the question immediately.

'Hmmmm,' 'How did you make him play at this level? Didn't it bother you?' Tiwari threw another question like a journalist.

'Uncle, actually I had seen him in the matches at local level. He is in our school. I convinced my P. T. I. sir about him, and he left the decision on me,' Bunty replied.

'Bunty, do you realise what a good job you have done, my boy,' Khandekar gave a heavy pat on Bunty's shoulder. Nitin was listening to their conversation.

'What does your father do Nitin?, Dharmendra Tiwari turned up to Nitin.

'Sir, he works in Saraswati Girls School,' Nitin replied.

'What subject does he teach?

'Sir, he is a peon there,' Nitin's innocent reply brought made one of the richest businessmen of Kanpur city to become serious. Either Nitin's reply made him realise that being a millionaire doesn't guarantee your son to be extraordinarily talented, or, made him feel poor in front of a son of a peon.

'Don't worry, whenever you require anything, just come to my house without any hesitation. OK. Dharmendra said with a fake smile.

'OK, sir.'

'By the way, we all should move to the pavilion because Nitin is sweating a lot,' Tiwari said, wiping his face with a handkerchief. All the boys started to follow the front line in which Nitin, Bunty, Tiwari and Khandekar were walking simultaneously.

'Nitin, you have to come to Green Park daily for practice from next week,' Deepak Khandekar said as all reached in.

'But sir, I will have to take permission from my father,' Nitin replied with innocence.

'Don't worry, I will talk to him.'

'How far is Green Park from your house?'

'Sir, it takes almost forty minutes on bicycle. The distance is about fifteen km between both the places,' Bunty intervened in the conversation.

'Hmmmm,' Khandekar looked at the ceiling of the big room.

Sir, if his father agrees, I can drop him at the ground as I come here to take tuition in maths daily.' Vishal's words brought a big smile on Khandekar's face.

'But, how will you stay here till seven,' Khandekar put up a valid question and Bunty became serious.

'It's OK, let's see what can be done,' Khandekar said after a pause of almost forty seconds. The players interrupted their conversation.

'Hey, what happened? What score did S. P. School make?'

'Sir, we bowled them out for 165,' captain Rakesh from hostel team replied.

'You should be ashamed of yourself, Rakesh. Despite having U. P.' s best bowlers, you threw away such runs.'

'Sorry, sir.'

'What sorry, when this news gets published in tomorrow's newspaper, it will be tough for me to have an eye to eye contact with the local coaches and U.P.C.A. officials,' Khandekar scolded him in front of the remaining boys.

'Just go and tell your openers that they both have to finish the match in less than twenty five overs. Otherwise, they will not be able to bat in the net for the entire week.'

'OK sir,' Rakesh replied looking shattered.

SEVEN

'Mummy, look at this and read it,' Reena entered the house with joy. She was carrying a newspaper in her hand.

'What happened?' Savitri asked while hanging a wet cloth on the wire that was attached to the wall.

'Look mom, Nitin's photo has been published in Dainik Jagran and Amar Ujala newspapers.'

'What! Where?' Savitri threw the wet shirt in the tub and rushed to catch the newspaper.

'Your son has made you proud in the entire locality. Just look at this and read it,' Reena showed the second last page of Dainik Jagran to her mother. The news was published in the left-upper column along with Nitin's photo in the headlines: Green Park hostel crushed S. P. College by eight wickets, but Nitin won the hearts.

'When did he play the match?' Savitri asked with eyes wide open.

'Don't act mummy. Both of us know very well that Nitin goes to play daily despite our locking the door and hiding the keys,' Reena said with a smile.

'But, for last three days I have been keeping the keys with myself.'

'Then how did he play yesterday? Have Jagran and Amar_Ujala published old news?' Reena laughed after thinking for a while.

'Look at his dress Reena. He is in white dress. He does not have any white dress as well,' Savitri's eyes became more wide.

'Oh yes, you are right mummy,' Reena gave the same expression as her mother.

'Yesterday, when he came back home with Vishal, he had worn black pants and green T-shirt,' Savitri said, thinking with her eyes closed. The newspaper was still in her hand.

'Hmmm, everything seems to be a mystery,' Reena said.

'Check once agains. Is this really our Nitin or someone else?'

'Come on mom, you are not so old that you can't recognise your own son.'

'We should wake him up. He is sleeping till now. He will tell the truth himself.' Both of them rushed inside the room.

'Hey, Nitin, get up,' Reena said loudly and shook Nitin.

'Yes, what is the matter?' Nitin asked yawning. 'Get up and look at this newspaper. Your photo has been published.'

'Where is my photo?' Nitin sat immediately and his laziness disappeared.

'Is this your photo?' This time the mother intervened loudly as Nitin was watching closely.

'Yes,' Nitin said with nervousness.

'Then, why are you afraid? Say loudly that this is your photo. By the way, yesterday you had worn black pant and green T-shirt but, your photo is in white,' Savitri asked, staring at him.

'Actually, mummy, yesterday there was a big match in the Green Park stadium. Since I did not have white dress, Vishal arranged it for me,' Nitin said with innocence.

'Hmmm, don't worry. I will give you a new white dress before your next match.'

'But, papa,'

Now, I'll see how he stops you from playing cricket. Don't worry about it,' Savitri said rubbing his head.

Yes! Nitin almost jumped off the bed and embraced his mother.'

'Yes, whom do you want to meet?, Savitri asked as she opened the gate. It was 10 am when somebody knocked the gate.

'Is this Mr. Seetaram's house?' a gentleman, around forty five year old, asked.

'Yes,' Savitri replied.

'Is he inside?' asked the gentleman.

'Yes, he is.' Savitri replied.

'I am Deepak Khandekar. I am the senior cricket coach in the Green Park cricket ground.'

'Oh! Please come in,' Savitri made way for him to come in.

'Seetaram *ji*, I am the senior cricket coach in Green Park. Where is Nitin?' After a few minutes Deepak Khandekar gave his introduction again while sitting in an old plastic chair.

'He is sleeping right now. I will wake him up.'

'Leave it. No need to wake him as I have come to talk to you only. I will talk to him later,' Deepak replied.

'OK, tell me what can I do for you?' Savitri was listening with great attention.

'You also sit please,' Deepak requested Savitri to sit on the bed.

'OK, sir,' Savitri replied.

'Seetaram *ji,* have you seen yesterday's newspaper?' Deepak looked up at Seetaram.

'No, what happened?'

'Sir, I have seen it, and read it all,' Savitri's face glittered with smile as she understood the matter.

'I have come here to talk about your son, Deepak Khandekar. said.

'Is there anything serious?' Seetaram asked.

'Yes, you can say that. I want to tell you that you son has a special talent,' Khandekar said after looking at the floor for almost thirty seconds.

'What do you want to say? I didn't understand.' Seetaram expressed.

'Seetaram *ji*, your son has a special talent. You should send him to Green Park daily for practice,' Seetaram looked at Savitri.

'Sir,' Seetaram looked at Deepak, but his words couldn't come out of his mouth.

'Seetaram *ji*, if he became's a superstar, all your problems will come to an end. You can spend your remaining life in a bungalow, and move around in expensive cars.' Khandekar said with twinkling eyes.

'Sir, let me tell you that as far as I remember, no one has held a bat amongst my ancestors.'

'Seetaram *ji*, trust me, one day you will be a proud father. Let me tell you that day after tomorrow Kanpur zones' under-sixteen team trial is going to take place. But, I have already selected him in the team. Do you understand how big it is?' Seetaram kept listening and staring at Deepak Khandekar.

'It means that Nitin will have to go out of the city as well to participate in matches,' Savitri intervened this time.

'Yes, coincidentally Kanpur under-sixteen team has to go to Meerut. Uttar Pradesh's all zonal teams will play matches in Meerut and, U.P's under-sixteen team will be selected on the basis of their performance in those matches.'

'Sir, give us time to think, we will let you know by tomorrow,' Savitri said.

'Yes, you take your own time but, do send Nitin, day after tomorrow to participate in the selection trial. It's just a formality.'

'Sure, sir, we will send him,' answered Seetaram.

'Good morning, sir. How did you know my address?' Nitin woke up and joined in the conversation.

'It was not a tough job, my son, to find out your address. By the way, I have come to say that you have to come at Green Park hostel day after tomorrow. You must reach before 10 a.m.

'Is there any match, sir?'

'No, it's trial of Kanpur under-sixteen. I have told Vishal. He will take care of everything.

'OK, sir,' Nitin replied.

'Seetaram *ji*, I should move now and no need to worry.' Deepak Khandekar got up from the chair and folded his hands.

* * *

Almost after a week, Nitin and his family members were quite busy, as in the evening he had to leave for Meerut to participate in the Zonal under-sixteen tournament.' Have you put in all your stuff in the bag?' Savitri asked loudly. 'Yes, mom,' Nitin replied.

'I have put in four trousers and shirts,' his sister said loudly while rolling the barrel on the bread in kitchen.

'When will your coach come?' Nitin's mother asked.

'He will come at 6:30 p.m.' Nitin replied.

'Will the train depart at 7:00 p.m. ?'

'Yes', Nitin said.

'OK, then you can take rest for some time as few hours are left. Your coach will come after four hours.

'No, I will watch Jatin's batting highlights as ESPN channel is about to start a special programme on him from today and that, too, just after fifteen minutes.' Nitin went inside the room after gazing at the wall clock.

'Yes, where is Nitin?' Almost after three hours Deepak Khandekar was beating the door of Seetaram's house and crying out in a loud voice.

'Yes sir, please come in. We were waiting for you,' Savitri said, opening the door.

'Thanks.' Deepak entered the house.

'Sir, please wait for five to ten minutes as he is offering prayers,' Seetaram intervened.

'Oh, that's great!' Seetaram's words made him curious. He went in to the next room and started watching Nitin closely. As he reached close to Nitin, Deepak's eyes got stuck on a photo which was put in a small window, adjacent to Lord *Ganesha* (Hindu God). Having seen that photo, Deepak looked at Savitri, who was standing just few steps back. She smiled back at Deepak, while he was overwhelmed.

'You worship Jatin,' Deepak asked with surprise as Nitin finished his prayers and opened his eyes.

'Sir, he is my ideal, and my God,' Nitin said.

'Keep it up this spirit, my son,' Deepak rubbed his hand with affection on Nitin's hair.

'OK, be quick and put your bag in the car's back seat. We have to leave for the station as soon as possible,' Deepak Khandekar checked the time in his wrist watch. Within minutes, Nitin picked up the bag and rushed outside.

'Stop for a minute. Touch your parents' feet before sitting in the car,' Deepak told Nitin.

'OK, sir,' Nitin touched his parents' feet one by one. Both, Seetaram and Savitri, hugged him and kissed on his cheek having tears in their eyes. Same was done by Reena also. Soon, the car went out of sight.

EIGHT

Two day later.

'*Mom*, just look at this,' Reena entered the room while reading the newspaper.

'What happened? Why are you crying so much?' Savitri scolded her as she was offering prayers.

'Look at the newspaper, mom. Nitin's photo has been published,' Reena replied.

'Show me,' Savitri snatched the newspaper from Reena.

'Wonder boy Nitin *ke dohre shatak ne kiya Meerut ko tahas-nahas* (Wonder boy Nitin's double century destroyed Meerut).' The headlines were written on the upper right portion of the column along with the photo of Nitin. Savitri "gulped" every single word of the news through her eyes.

'He is my son. I am proud of my son,' Savitri said in a loud voice after reading the news.

'Look at this and read it. You always keep scolding my son,' Savitri threw the newspaper at Seetaram as he entered the room with a jug of milk in one hand.

'What are you doing? The jug will fall,' Seetaram said. He immediately gave the jug of milk to Reena and started reading the news.

'Now, promise me that you will never stop Nitin from playing cricket and not scold him unnecessarily,' Savitri said as Seetaram finished reading the news.

'OK, I will not scold him.' Seetaram replied.

NINE

After ten days.

'Who is jumping on the roof?' Savitri jabbered in sleep. She was lying in bed along with Reena. It was around 1:30 a.m.

'Reena, hey Reena,' Savitri shook her.

'What's up, mom? Don't bother me please,' Reena replied and jolted mother's hand.

'Hey, get up,' Savitri shook Reena again.

'What happened? Why are you teasing me in the night?' Reena said.

'After all......'

'Shhhhhhh....' Savitri shut Reena's mouth with her hand. Reena became a little serious.

'It seems to me that someone is on the roof. Can you hear the sound?' Savitri said in a low voice.

'Yes, definitely, someone is there. Lest it should be a thief,' Reena said. This time her face was gripped with fear.

'We should wake up papa,' Reena said.

'Yes, and turn on the switch of the tube light carefully as Nitin is lying on the floor,' Savitri said.

'Hey, where is Nitin?' Both spoke simultaneously with surprise as soon as the tube light was switched on. Both looked inside the inner room and in the corridor as well, including the roof. But they didn't find Nitin anywhere. The worry of missing Nitin had replaced the worry for the sound they heard a few minutes back.

'Mom, I feel that the sound is coming from outside.' Both of them rushed downstairs.

'Oh, the lock is already open,' Reena said as she found that the door was unlocked. As soon as they came out of the house, their eyes got wide open. Nitin was skipping under the flood light which was just on the left side of house. He was sweating badly, and had worn two pair of pads. The sound was echoing in the dim light.

'2001... 2002... 2003...Nitin was counting the numbers with each skip. Sometimes, the rope was sticking with his feet, and in between he was taking two to three skips under each jump at regular intervals. Seeing that, Savitri became emotional and tears started rolling down her cheeks. Reena tried to move ahead, but Savitri stopped her by holding her hand.

'Shhhhhh...Let him do his austerities. Don't disturb him. We will talk to him tomorrow.' Both, Reena and Savitri left Nitin and returned inside. Both lay down on the bed and kept listening the the sound with open eyes almost for next half an hour, till Nitin came back in the room. None of them disturbed Nitin and he went into the adjacent room to sleep.

Same day

8:00 a.m.

'Hey Nitin, get up and drink your milk,' Savitri was standing near Nitin's bed with a glass of milk. Suddenly, she saw a drawing sheet put up by the bedside. She kept the glass of milk on the table and tried to read by bending forward. There were at least ten half sheets stuck on the supporting plywood. She kept looking at those for almost five minutes and tried her best to read the words but, she couldn't read any except the one which was written in Hindi. It read, "*Mujhe ek din Jatin Tendulkar banna hai* (One day I have to become Jatin)"

On the remaining sheets, words were written in English, "I have to play for India just like Jatin played. I have to become a better batsman than Jatin. I have to play for the Indian team before I turn sixteen" 'Hey Nitin, get up and drink your milk,' Savitri shook him with force this time.

'Yes, *mom,* 'Nitin got up snoozing.

'Take your *parantha* (fried bread) and milk,' Savitri said.

'How did this happen?' Savitri asked when she saw swelling and clots on Nitin's legs while he drank the milk.

'Nothing, *mummy*, the ball hit me when I was batting,' Nitin replied.

'By the way, what were you doing outside last night?'

'Did you see me?' He asked with surprise.

'Yes, and Reena too,' replied Savitri.

'It's called skipping *mummy*. It's done to strengthen the legs.

'But, why during the night?'

'Actually, nowadays, I am not going to the ground for fitness, so I thought night is the right time for skipping as people keep passing by daytime,' Nitin replied.

'But, you did all this for more than an hour, and you had even worn something on your legs…what are those called?' Savitri said recollecting with her eyes closed.

'Pads,' said Nitin.

'Whatever it is,' Savitri said.

'It must be very painful,' she said having taken pause for a few seconds.

'When Jatin was of my age, he used to skip ten thousand times in a day, that too, without taking any break,' said Nitin. 'Who told you this?' asked Savitri.

'Senior players keep talking about this in the ground. They narrate so many stories about Jatin. I have to work even harder than him if I have to play for India before the age he played.' Nitin emphasised on the last line with his fists closed tightly. Zest and passion could be felt easily in his body language.

'May God give you success in your hard work and may your dream come true my son. You are the hope of our family.' Savitri became emotional.

'I will leave no stone unturn in my hard work mom,' Nitin replied.

'But give attention to your diet,' Savitri said loudly after coming out of her emotions.

'OK mom, I will,' Nitin said.

TEN

One year later.

'What are you doing, Kapil? You have wasted another opportunity,' Dharmendra Tiwari, chairman of Kanpur Cricket Association gave rebuke to his son, in his house.

'Papa, that specific ball kept low,' Kapil explained.

'Batting is a matter of only one ball. One ball is enough to finish your life. How long will I keep backing you?' Dharmendra said.

'Papa, I will play a big knock soon,' Kapil promised.

'I have been listening to this for a year now. I have given you the best facilities. You play with the best equipments in the entire Uttar Pradesh. The driver drops you and picks you from the ground daily but, what have you done?' Dharmendra looked angry.

'Sorry papa, I will try my best,' Kapil reassured.

'I want to see you play for India, my son but you are leaving no stone unturned in fading out my dreams. Just look at this and read it. Where has a peon's son reached in a year?' Dharmendra Tiwari threw the newspaper at Kapil's face in anger. Newspaper fell down after hitting his face. "Nitin's ton won the Rajeev Gandhi cup for the Kanpur Greens" The headline was published on the sports page of the National English daily, along with Nitin's photo. And, it served like a punch to the father-son duo.

'You have been selected in the state under-sixteen team. But, if you don't score runs, then it will be tough even for me to back you,' Dharmendra showed concern.

'Don't worry, papa. In this session I will beat Nitin,' Kapil assured his father once again.

'Stop scoring by words. It is high time you scored with your bat,' Tiwari said, staring at Kapil.

'Sorry, papa,' Kapil apologised.

The door bell rang.

'Check it out. Surely, it is the peon's son,' Dharmendra said after looking at his wrist watch.

'Why has he come?' Kapil asked looking surprised.

'He has come for a kit-bag. He had requested for it yesterday after the match,' Dharmendra replied.

'You go inside and hide. Don't come out until he leaves, OK,' Dharmendra Tiwari said after taking a pause.

'OK, *papa*,' Kapil went inside.

'Good evening, sir,' Nitin wished Dharmendra as he opened the door.

'Hey Nitin, how are you? Please come in,' Dharmendra ushered Nitin inside.

'Thank you, sir,' Nitin entered the room of a huge bungalow.

'Yesterday, you really played well. You made a fantastic hundred.' Soon, Nitin was sitting in a large room with Dharmendra. Dharmendra's words were not matching the expressions on his face.

'Thanks a lot, sir.' Nitin gave a smile.

'Now, tell me, what have you come for?' Dharmendra peeped through the glasses.

'Sir, I told you yesterday. As you know that U.P. under-sixteen team will be leaving for Punjab after a week, hence, I require a good bat as my bat is almost broken,' Nitin said with hesitation.

'Did you talk to Deepak Khandekar?'

'Yes, sir, actually, he uses a very long bat,' Nitin answered.' Hmmmm.'

Dharmendra started to meditate with his eyes closed and both his hands were resting behind the head.

'My son, just two days back, I had two brand new bats but one is taken by a close friend, and the other one by a relative,' Dharmendra told Nitin.

'No problem, sir. Even if you have an old one, it's OK.' Nitin confirmed.

'My son, I have old bats but, all are too long one and not suitable for you. Don't worry, I will tell Kapil to share his bat with you,' said Dharmendra.

'But, sir, he uses a heavy bat, and his bat doesn't suit my technique,' Nitin argued.

'Then, I am sorry, my son,' Dharmendra said.

'It's OK, sir. Thanks.' Nitin folded his hands and left the house with a sad face.

* * *

'Hey, Vishal, I am fed up of begging a bat from others,' Nitin told Vishal as they met in the evening in a park, in front of Vishal's house.

'I, too, don't like that you keep begging people like Dharmendra. He will never give you anything as he is jealous of you,' Vishal said.

'I went to his house because he had told me that whenever I require his help, I could go to him,' Nitin said.

'I know he said that long time back in everybody's presence, when you played your first match in Green Park. But now, he compares his son with you. Why will he give you a bat?' Vishal said.

'Fuck off, this bat had to be broken even this time,' Nitin said while throwing a piece of stone in anger.

'Be cool. You will gain nothing by showing anger. It's time to do something,' Vishal said.

'What's the price of a new bat?' Vishal asked.

'It's almost five thousand rupees,' Nitin replied.

'Do you have money?' Vishal asked.

'Around fifteen hundred rupees, and it's too less to purchase a bat,' Nitin said feeling dejected.

'I have around two thousand rupees with me,' offered Vishal.

'But where will remaining fifteen hundred come from?' Nitin asked.

'Don't worry, dear. Arrangement will be done,' Vishal replied.

'How?' Nitin stared at him.

'Look at that,' Vishal pointed out.

'What is that?' Nitin asked in curiosity.

'That is Firoz *bhai's* shop,' Vishal replied.

'Will Firoz *bhai* arrange the remaining money for my bat?' Nitin enquired.

'Yes, indeed, he will,' Vishal said.

'Have you gone mad?' Nitin said in anger and irritation.

'No, have a look at that big piece of iron,' Vishal pointed out.

'The one on which he beats his scarps? 'Nitin asked.

'Yes, that piece of iron will give us money,' Vishal said, smiling.

'Are you planning to steal that big piece of iron?', Nitin asked.

'Yes, absolutely,' replied Vishal.

'But that is not a good thing to do,' Nitin said.

'We have no other option, Nitin. Presently, we have to arrange a bat at any cost,' Vishal said in a loud voice, which made Nitin calm and compelled him to think.

'But, it's very heavy. It doesn't seem to be less than fifty kilos,' Nitin reiterated.

'It's more than fifty kilos but, don't worry. What you have to do is to just keep an eye on the people from your roof night. If anyone seems to be coming from either side, you have to whistle, OK?' Vishal put his hand on Nitin's shoulder.

'OK, but, how will you do that?' Nitin showed concern.

'I have already spoken to a scrapper. Many rickshaw-pullers keep their vehicles in our compound on rent everyday. I have thought about everything. You just go now and get ready at 11:00 p.m.,' Vishal said.

'OK, thank you very much, Vishal.' Both departed. Exactly at 11:00 p.m., Nitin was on the roof of his house for Vishal's help. Both did their job successfully without facing any problem.

ELEVEN

Two day later.

7.00 pm

Seetaram went to Kanpur railway station to drop Nitin as U.P. under-sixteen team was going to leave for Punjab in half an hour.

'Have you packed-up all your stuff?' Seetaram asked Nitin. 'Yes, *papa*. I have already checked the bag twice,' Nitin replied.

'Hmmm, take and put these into your bag.' Seetaram gave ten notes of hundred rupees to Nitin. 'Put these in your bag, or, should I give these to Khandekar sir?, Seetaram asked.

'Don't worry, *papa*. I am good enough to handle that. I am grown up now,' Nitin said, keeping the money in his pocket.

Hey Nitin, move quickly. Sir is calling you.' Kapil's voice disrupted the conversation.

'OK *papa*, I should move as we have to assemble and check our berth as well,' Nitin touched Seetaram's feet and rushed towards the group of remaining boys who were standing almost hundred meters away from them.

'OK, my son. Take care of yourself and make good scores.' Seetaram rubbed Nitin's head.

After Half and hour.

'Hey Nitin, you are the biggest hope for our team,' Kapil said. Around seven to eight boys were talking to each other, sitting on the lower berth. Others were sleeping or reading books.

'Hey, don't do buttering,' Nitin replied while reading a book.

'Now, where is the question of buttering? You are the highest run scorer in U.P. state tournaments, that too in all age categories.

Am I saying anything wrong Rohit?' Kapil tried to get support from Rohit, who was lying in Nitin's lap.

'Yes, that's right,' Rohit replied.

'What's right?' Kapil asked.

'Nitin is the highest run scorer.' Rohit replied.

'Hey *saale*, I am talking about the comment,' Kapil said.

'I didn't listen,' Rohit said with a smile.

'Why will you listen, *saale*? You have been his follower.' Kapil hit on Rohit's leg.

'Then, why are you asking me? Don't hit me or else I will break your teeth,' Rohit got up and pointed out to Kapil shouting.

Hey, why are you fighting? It's not even half an hour that we boarded the train and you have started fighting,' Nitin intervened.

'Make him understand, Nitin. He should know whom he is talking to?' Kapil said. Some boys were silent listeners, and others were enjoying the fight.

'*Beta*, I have been selected because of my performance, not through "*Jugad*",' Rohit fired at Kapil.

'What did you say *saale*?' Kapil got up from his seat to catch Rohit but Nitin caught him and made him sit, forcefully.

'Calm down, Kapil Tiwari, be cool,' Nitin said and put the book aside.

'Hey, you are reading a book on Jatin', Kapil picked up the book as he saw Jatin's picture on the cover page.

'Let me finish first', Nitin tried to snatch it back.

'I will only see Jatin's pictures. Please give me five minutes,' Kapil requested.

'OK, but not more than five minutes as I have to finish this book before midnight,' Nitin said.

'Hey, from where did you get Jatin's autograph?' Kapil's eyes became wide as he turned the cover page. On the third page, there was a huge autograph. Kapil Tiwari's loud voice alerted the remaining boys. Almost all of them stopped their work and gathered around

Kapil to see the autograph. Nitin smiled as if a huge mystery was hidden behind the autograph.

'It's my signature, not of Jatin,' Nitin said.

'I can't believe this. It's absolutely similar to Jatin's,' Kapil looked stunned.

'Yes, this is my signature. It took me almost a year to copy Jatin's signature. One day, I have to become a big star like Jatin,' Nitin said while looking at the wall of the compartment.

'Fuck off. I will never let you become like Jatin,' Kapil spoke in his mind.

'Great! I will pray for you,' Kapil said, and the remaining boys took their seats again.

'Hey, what is this?' Kapil asked, dragging Nitin's locket close to himself. The locket was carrying a small bat and a key.

'This was given by my sister Reena on *Bhaiya-dauj*.' Nitin said.

'Really! It's fantastic. It seems to be made of gold,' Kapil said while sneering at the bat but, his eyes were following the key, rather than the bat.

'No, it's made of silver. It has been polished with gold,' Nitin replied.

'Nice one, nice one.' Kapil was still looking at the bat.

'Leave it and see the picture soon as I have to finish the book.' Nitin took his locket off Kapil's hand.

2:35 a.m.

Kapil got up and looked around closely. There was absolutely dark inside the coach and all the passengers were in deep sleep. He got up from the seat and walked towards the toilet. Almost after five minutes, he returned and bent down towards Nitin, who was snoring loudly, and his locket was hanging towards the floor. Kapil took the locket out of Nitin's neck. Having taken the key out of locket, he put the locket in the pocket of his half pant. He again bent after observing the situation closely by looking around. Within minutes, Kapil unlocked Nitin's kit-bag, which was tied with the lower-birth through a thick iron chain. Having done his job, Kapil put the key back in the locket, and soon, locket was hanging in Nitin's neck the way it was earlier.

Kapil started crawling towards the toilet again, which was, coincidently, very close to those seats where other boys were sleeping. He observed every passenger very closely, they were either snoring or were in the lap of deep sleep. After coming out from the toilet, Kapil opened the gate of the compartment and sat near it to soak his sweat. Having felt the breeze for almost three to four minutes, he returned to his seat, observing the passengers again. He picked up Nitin's kit-bag with both his hands and came to the gate. He caught the gate with one hand and, with the other hand, he threw Nitin's kit-bag out of the gate. The bag was lost in darkness. Though, tension and fear gripped his face and dribbles of sweat were exuding, Kapil did what he had planned out a few hours back. After closing the gate of the bogie, he returned softly to his seat and lay down on the lower berth.

'Hey, get up...get up boys, we are reaching the Ludhiana station in ten minutes,' Rohit called out loudly by shaking all the boys. Within minutes, all boys swung into action, except Nitin and Kapil.

'How far is the station?' Nitin babbled in sleep.

'Get up, Nitin, all the passengers are up,' Rohit shook Nitin and Kapil again. Nitin got up yawning.

'Hey Nitin, have your tea. Your laziness will go within minutes,' Rohit said.

'Wait for two minutes,' Nitin said while getting up in order to wear his footwear.

'Hey Rohit, where is my kit bag?' As Nitin looked at the floor, his face turned pale.

'My kit-bag is stolen,' Nitin started crying loudly. All boys were shocked and gathered around Nitin.

'What are you all doing here? Search the whole bogie and inform Khandekar sir. Be quick.' Kapil scolded the boys and they scattered in the compartment in search of that kit bag, which was never going to be found. One boy rushed to the next compartment to inform Deepak Khandekar. While Rohit was consoling Nitin, he was crying loudly.

'What will I do Rohit? Somehow I had managed a brand new bat,' Nitin said.

'Don't worry. Everything will be all right,' Rohit consoled him.

'Hmmmm, it means that the kit bag was stolen when the train stopped at one of the last few stations.' Deepak Khandekar said after inspecting the chain, and the place, where the bag was kept. Nitin was sobbing badly.

'Boys, move quickly as our station has come,' Khandekar said in a loud voice as the train stopped.

TWELVE

Fourteen days later.

Celebration was in its full colour in a hotel room, more for Nitin's not out double ton than U.P. team's entry in the knock-out round.

'Hey Nitin, you are a rock star. Take one more bite; 'No, it's enough', Nitin tried to stop him 'Please eat as I too have given contribution in your double ton'.

'How?', Nitin asked with surprise.

Did I give contribution, or not?'. Kapil said while forcefully cramming a piece of cake into Nitin's mouth. Some boys had pasted the cream of cake on Nitin's face as well. 'You made double ton with my bat.

'Ha-ha, you are right. You have given contribution in my double ton'. Nitin surprise turned in to laughter and he took another piece in to his mouth from his hand.

'Well done! Nitin. I am really proud of you.' Deepak Khandekar, too, put a piece of cake into Nitin's mouth.

'Thank you, sir,' Nitin said, touching his feet.

'Sir, he does good mimicry as well', Rohit intervened.

'Oh Really! Whose mimicry does he do?' Deepak asked.

'Sir, Jatin Tendulkar's,' Rohit replied with a smile.

'I will love to see it. Some of you can sit on the bed and some on the floor, please, 'Khandekar said while mashing his palm against each other.

'No, sir, Rohit is telling a lie,' Nitin replied bashfully.

'I know who is telling a lie. Start the act quickly and all the boys will also do something alike.' ordered Deepak.

Soon, Nitin started to act like Jatin. He enacted one of the TV commercial Jatin's.

'Wonderful, Nitin, wonderful! You did a fantastic act.' Khandekar gave a standing ovation while clapping. After Nitin, all the sixteen boys performed different things like dance, singing etc.

'OK, boys, I have to move out. It's 9 p.m. now. You all have to go to bed by 10 p.m. You have to practice hard for the knock-out match against Mumbai. So you have only one more hour to have fun,' Deepak said.

'OK, sir,' many sounds echoed simultaneously.

Deepak Khandekar left the room.

'Yes, now it will be real celebration,' Kapil immediately rushed to lock the room from inside.

'No, I will not take part in this game,' Nitin said.

'Why are you throwing tantrums? Today is a big day and it calls for real celebration,' Rohit said loudly.

'Let us start the game.' As Rohit said this, one boy rushed to switch off the tube light. Within seconds, many sounds started echoing; "Save yourself"..."Hide yourself under the bed"..."Lay down on the floor". It was obvious that "footwear game" was catching pace. In the dark, the footwear was hitting on someone's back and sometimes on the other part of the body, room, wall, etc. This game continued for a long time amidst laughter and painful voice, until a very loud cry echoed.

'*Mom*...*Mom*,' Nitin started crying loudly. Even in the dark, Kapil Tiwaris' well planned throw hit the bull's eye. Nitin sat down crying loudly and covered his right eye with his hand.

'Stop...stop...switch on the lights please.' As Rohit said, all the boys stopped and gathered around Nitin.

'Remove your hand Nitin. Let me see your eye,' Rohit said, but Nitin was crying badly. Some boys made Nitin sit on the bed.

'Oh my God!' As Rohit took Nitin's hand off his right eye, he saw a big blood clot in Nitin's eye, and there was huge swelling, as well, around his eyes.

'Who is the bastard?' Rohit cried.

'There is no point shouting now. We should rush to a doctor or nursing home,' Kapil intervened.

'Be quick. Arrange for a vehicle or rickshaw,' Rohit said and took Nitin out of the room by putting his right hand on his eye.

'Hey, what happened?' the receptionist, a thirty five years old man, shouted as he saw a group of boys coming downstairs.

'He has got a severe injury and we have to take him to the doctor,' Rohit said.

'But, how? Where is your coach?' the receptionist asked.

'He has gone to meet his friend.' Rohit replied.

'It's Ok. I'll arrange for a car. Only two to three boys come along with Nitin,' the receptionist said.

Within five minutes, Nitin, Rohit and Kapil Tiwari, along with the receptionist, moved out in a car on the wide roads of Ludhiana.

* * *

'You all have fucked the team's aspiration,' Khandekar scolded the boys who were standing in a line with heads bowed down.

'Bastards, all of you come on to your knees. You have to be in the same position for an hour.' All the boys immediately came on their knees as Khandekar cried.

'Why, at all, did you involve Nitin in this game? Had he not been injured, I would have given him the same punishment,' Khandekar said pointing towards Nitin, who was lying. His eye was covered with a bandage. By then Nitin had slept.

'Doctor, everything is up to you now. He is our best player. All our national selectors are coming to see Nitin's game. Only you can make him fit,' with a worried face, Deepak Khandekar told the doctor, who was removing Nitin's bandage in the hotel room.

'I will try my best, sir,' the doctor replied.

'Oh my God, so much swelling,' Deepak said with surprise as the doctor took the bandage off.

'Will he be normal by tomorrow morning as he has to play a very crucial match?' Khandekar asked, as the doctor was busy inspecting Nitin's eye.

'I have written the medicines. Take them on time and, let's pray and hope.' Doctor handed over the paper to Khandekar.

'OK, sir, I should move. And yes, give a gentle massage around his eye for one hour at least.' The doctor gave a light pat on Deepak's shoulder. Soon, the doctor left the room.

6:00 a.m.

'My son, if you play, then the condition of your eye will worsen,' Deepak Khandekar was convincing Nitin not to play the match as swelling around his eye was still the same as on the previous night.

'Sir, I am fit enough to play the match,' Nitin replied.

'Have you looked at yourself in the mirror? Swelling is still the same,' Khandekar cried. It was more of his frustration than anger.

'I have seen, sir. Come what may, I will play,' Nitin insisted.

'But, it will be tough in the helmet. Sweat will make it even worse,' Khandekar warned.

'I will play without the helmet, sir' Nitin replied.

'Have you gone mad? What will happen if the ball hits at the same spot?' Khandekar cried out loudly.

'Don't worry, sir, nothing will happen to me,' Nitin replied.

'I am very afraid, my son.' Khandekar caught Nitin's hand.

'Don't be afraid, sir, everything is going to be fine.' Nitin's eyes were glittering with confidence.

* * *

'All the boys go in and receive him,' as Khandekar gave the order and rushed towards the ground, all the boys followed him. Just after the third day of injury, Nitin was returning with 136 not out inning, taking his team into semifinal. As Khandekar reached close to him, he lifted Nitin and made him sit on his shoulder. All the boys were following him and only one voice kept echoing for next few minutes, "Nitin"..."Nitin"..."Nitin".

The noise took the shine off Kapil face, who was pretending to be happy among the boys.

THIRTEEN

Fifteen days later.

'It's a very proud moment for the whole colony that we have such a big talent in the form of Nitin,' a gentleman was giving speech in a function. It was organised in the honour of Nitin by the local society as he got selected in India under-sixteen team.

'Nitin has not only made our locality proud, but also the whole Kanpur also,' clapping echoed for a few minutes until a man walked up on the stage.

'I would request the chief of Kanpur Cricket Association and the chairman of our society, Mr. Dharmendra Tiwari, to please up and give a momento to Nitin.' The sound of clapping became almost three times louder as Nitin got off the chair in the front row. At the same time, Dharmendra Tiwari also stood up in Nitin's honour.

'I am proud of you, Nitin,' Tiwari said while handing over the trophy to Nitin. Almost hundred people were clapping for him.

'Thank you, sir.' After ten minutes, everyone was having breakfast. People were chatting in groups and Nitin was the star among all. Nitin was taking breakfast with his friends. Suddenly, somebody gave a light pat on his shoulder from behind.

'Hello, Nitin, autograph please.' Nitin turned back and kept looking for a while. His friends were smiling. This was Shalu, the locality's most beautiful and intelligent girl of the colony not only amongst boys and girls of her age but also the senior as well. She had won many awards at the city level in debates, writing and other competitions. As a result of her achievement at such a young age, everyone respected her. She was the dream girl of most of the boys in the locality.

'Hey, why are you feeling shy? I am asking for your autograph,' Shalu remarked.

'Give your autograph, Nitin,' Vishal said.

'I am not such a big player,' Nitin replied.

'By the way, I am Shalu Gupta. I live in the adjacent block', Shalu introduced herself to Nitin.

'Yes, I have seen you earlier,' Nitin replied.

'OK, can we be friends?' Shalu moved her hand forward.

'Hey, Shalu, what are you doing here? We were looking for you,' a voice took away all the attention before Nitin could shake hands. A gentleman, aged around forty five, along with Dharmendra Tiwari, came there.

'Papa, I was congratulating Nitin,' Shalu smiled.

'Why not, he is the future star,' Shalu's father replied.

'OK, Nitin, see you soon, bye-bye.' Having said that, Shalu left the place, but Nitin kept looking at her until she went out of sight.

FOURTEEN

Almost three month later.

'Hey Nitin, come quickly. Enough practice has been done now,' Shalu called Nitin from a distance of around hundred metres. Nitin was busy in the net practice with Vishal in Kamla Cricket Club Ground.

'Only last three balls left,' Nitin gave a reply by gesticulation.

'Why did you come here?' Nitin asked after taking his helmet off as he reached close to that bench, where Shalu was sitting.

'I wanted to see you practice,' Shalu said and gave a smile to Vishal.

'How did you know that we were here?' Nitin looked into Shalu's eyes.

'Actually, I used to see both of you, every second day, carrying a kit-bag, while going to school. I saw you even today, so I decided to come,' replied Shalu.

'Why did you bunk your class? You could have come after the last class was over,' Nitin said.

'What would I tell my mom then?' Shalu looked at Vishal as if she gave him a signal.

'OK, Nitin, I should move now,' Vishal said while looking at his wrist watch.

'Where are you going? I still have to bat.' Nitin looked at Vishal.

'I just recalled that I have to pick my sister from her tuition class. She must be waiting,' Vishal said.

'You didn't tell me anything in the morning,' Nitin asked politely.

'Sorry, I forgot,' Vishal answered.

'It's OK,' Nitin said.

'Bye-Bye Shalu. See you soon,' Vishal said looking at Shalu.

'Take the kit-bag along with you,' Nitin told Vishal.

'I will, there is no need to remind me.' Vishal put the kit-bag on his bike, and after few minutes, he left the ground.

'So, Nitin, what is going on?' Shalu broke the silence. It was a gap of hardly two feet between both of them on the bench.

'Nothing special dear. It has been only practice, and hard practice. I have to play the Ranji Trophy much before Jatin played in his age. I mean before fifteen years of age and 232 days,' Nitin gave stress on the last few words while looking into Shalu's eyes.

'It's OK, but don't forget that your exams are starting from next month,' Shalu reminded Nitin.

'I am paying equal attention to studies as well,' Nitin gave assurance.

'Good, keep it up. By the way, I have come for a special reason,' Shalu smiled.

'What reason ?' Nitin asked.

'I have something to give you,' Shalu replied.

'What?' Nitin smiled.

'Close your eyes,' Shalu told Nitin.

'But tell, what is that something?' Nitin insisted.

'No, first close your eyes.' Shalu closed his eyes with her hands.

'It's OK. It's OK,' Nitin took her hands off and closed his eyes.

'Don't open your eyes until I tell you to. OK,' Shalu bent and took out a small bag of polythene from her school bag.

'Happy Birthday to you...Happy Birthday to you, Nitin,' Shalu took out some stuff like a wrist watch, greeting card and a packet of sweets in her lap while singing those lines.

'Hey, what is this?' Instead of saying thanks, Nitin's eyes became wide with surprise.

'This is all for you, dear,' Shalu replied affectionately.

'What is the price of it?' Nitin picked up the wrist watch and looked at it carefully.

'Gifts are priceless. They have no price tag,' Shalu said.

'I know, but I am just asking for my knowledge,' Nitin blushed.

'Only fifteen hundred rupees,' Shalu said.

'Fifteen hundred rupees, such an expensive gift.' His eyes widened again.

'What expensive! last month I gifted a wrist watch worth six thousand rupees to my father on his birthday,' Shalu said casually.

'Hmmm,' Nitin ate a piece of sweet.

'I will have to hide it.' Nitin kept the watch in his pocket.

'Why?' Shalu asked.

'What will I say to my mom and sister?' Nitin expressed concern.

'Very easy, tell them that you got this as a reward for becoming the "Man of the Match". Shalu suggested.

'Yes, that is a good idea.' Nitin remarked.

'Hey look, something is stuck on your cheek,' Shalu said.

'What is it ?' He rubbed his hand on the cheek.

'Let me clean that,' Shalu stood up to clean the stuff but, instead of cleaning, she kissed on Nitin's cheek. Shalu's act left him blushing.

'Why are you blushing like girls?' Shalu remarked.

Nitin remained silent. He did'nt stop smiling though.

* * *

'Hey, Vishal, where are you coming from?' Kapil stopped his bike on the road as he saw Vishal.

'Hmmm, it seems that you are coming after playing a match,' Kapil spoke further even before Vishal could reply.

'I am coming from Kamla club. I had to bowl to Nitin.'

'Oh! This year, he will not take rest before getting selected for the Ranji Trophy,' Kapil made a comment.

'Yes, if he maintains good performance, the selectors would be compelled to pick him.'

'By the way, where is Nitin? You are alone,' Kapil said by looking around.

'Actually, he is in Kamla club as Shalu had come to meet him.'

'Shalu! but, why?' Kapil looked puzzeled.

'I don't know.' Vishal realised that he had made a mistake by making a mention about Shalu because she and Kapil were in the same class, but in different sections.

'OK, Vishal, bye. See you soon dear,' Kapil shook hands with him. Vishal started his bike while Kapil kept standing at the same place until Vishal became invisible. Kapil thought for few minutes and soon, he was on the way to Kamla club.

FIFTEEN

'Hey, plz eat one more piece,' Shalu said.

'Please, don't force me. I have already eaten so many,' replied Nitin.

'Last one, from my hand.' Shalu didn't wait for his reply and put the piece of sweet forcefully into Nitin's mouth. Shalu's act turned Kapil's face absolutely red. Kapil was standing behind the wall, which was hardly twenty to twenty five meters away from the bench, where Nitin and Shalu were sitting.

'OK, Nitin, I should make a move now and wish you a very happy birthday, again.' Shalu kissed on Nitin's face and this act made Kapil even more distressed.

'My throat is absolutely dry. Would you also like to drink something?' Nitin asked Shalu.

'Yes, I was about to tell you the same.' Both started walking straight. Soon, having walked around two hundred meter, both reached at drinking area.

'I am willing to take a bath,' Nitin said while drinking water from the tap.

'Yes, I am willing, too,' Shalu replied.

'Hey, why don't you fill your bottle? You have to go far,' Shalu remarked.

'Oh! My God, I forgot my bag under the bench,' Nitin recalled.

'You are the biggest fool in the world,' Shalu scolded him and both started runing towards the bench.

'Oh! My bag is stolen.' Nitin became weepy. Having done his job successfully, Kapil went away from there.

'It's very strange that the bag vanished within ten minutes,' Shalu said.

'It means that someone was keeping an eye on us.' Shalu walked around and looked at the back side of the wall, as well, where Kapil was hiding, but couldn't get any clue.

'My mom and sister will beat me!' Nitin sat on a bench and tears started rolling down his cheeks.

'What else will happen if you make such mistakes?' Shalu said with anger.

'By the way, don't worry. I will arrange the book for you.' Shalu spoke again.

'But, you are from English medium.'

'I have friends in Hindi medium as well.'

'How many books were in the bag?' Shalu asked.

'Four, including Maths and English along with the tuition register.' replied Nitin.

'Thank God, you didn't put the wrist watch and the greeting card in the bag. Otherwise, it would have been too embarrassing for me,' Shalu said.

'OK, don't be disappointed. Go back home and tell aunty that you left the bag at a friend's house because tuition class was postponed, OK?' Shalu said. Nitin got up and didn't say anything.

'OK, I will arrange the book. Meet me tomorrow at the same place. Bye.' Shalu hugged Nitin. Having kissed him one more time, she left the Kamla club, while Nitin kept mourning at the bench for next few minutes.

SIXTEEN

Ten days later.

'Hey, put up the balloons properly,' Kapil gave instructions to his friend in the class room during lunch break. Everyone was busy in decorating the classroom.

'Be quick guys, be quick. Break time will be over in twenty five minutes. Hey Sangeeta, fix this flotilla properly.' Being the second monitor of class, Kapil was observing the situation and giving instructions by going from one corner to another.

'Hey, what is the matter?' Shalu asked.

'It's a surprise. Just wait for ten minutes,' Kapil replied.

Shalu asked all her class mates, but all of them refused to answer.

'Go to hell, all of you.' Shalu left the class room. She felt insulted because she was the first monitor of the class, but no one was ready to share the matter with her.

'Hey Deepak, please go out and bring Shalu with you. You have five minutes,' Kapil ordered a fellow mate. Within five minutes, Shalu was in the classroom. All mates had taken the seat except Kapil Tiwari.

'What's the matter?' Shalu asked feeling annoyed.

'Actually, today is Mathur sir's marriage anniversary. So, we wanted to give him a surprise,' Kapil said.

'But, why did you hide all this from me?'

'There is a special reason behind it.'

'What's the special reason?' annoyance overpowered her words.

'Be cool and take this bouquet. Since you are the first monitor of class, we all want that you should give it to Mathur sir.' Kapil's statement brought smile on her face. Within minutes, Shalu was standing with the bouquet near the teacher's table.

'When will he come?' Shalu asked.

'You know that his class starts only once the lunch break is over.'

'It means, he will take around ten minutes as he always comes five to ten minutes late,' Shalu said while looking at her wrist watch.

'Saurabh,' Kapil said and a boy stood up and pushed the button on the board, which was hardly two feet from his reach. As he pushed the button, the ceiling fan started to buzz loudly. Flowers dropped straight on Shalu's head and only one voice was echoing in the entire class, "Happy Birthday to you"…. "Happy Birthday to you, Shalu"…. Shalu was speechless and stunned, but with a huge smile. All the students were standing and clapping.

'Thank you very much. You are very nice. I have no words for you. You all are my darling,' Shalu said.

'Shalu, you must thank Kapil for all this,' Deepak said, standing in the front row.

'Kapil Tiwari,' Shalu looked at Kapil with surprise, who was expecting to be praised by Shalu.

'Yes, Shalu, he bore the entire expense and told us not to disclose.'

'Come on, Kapil Tiwari, why did you do all this?' Soon the smile faded and she looked serious.

'Actually, you have been very dear to the entire class. So, we all wanted to celebrate your birthday in a special manner,' Kapil said.

'But then, why did you bear all the expenses? You should have collected the money from every student.' Shalu said.

'But….'

'No, Kapil Tiwari. It's wrong. What do you want to prove?' Shalu put the bouquet on the table.

'Sorry, Shalu,' Kapil said in a heavy tone.

'If you wanted to give a gift to me, you shouldn't have done this drama,' Shalu became angry again.

Kapil kept listening.

'Don't be angry, Shalu. He has done so much for you. You shouldn't behave in such a manner.' Deepak intervened.

'Shalu, we all love and respect you,' one girl's voice came from a corner.

'Yes....yes,' all students started shouting. It brought a smile on Shalu's face again. This was not a genuine smile. But, all this compelled her to shake hands with Kapil Tiwari.

'OK, Kapil Tiwari, Thanks for all this.' She hugged Kapil Tiwari, but half heartedly as she knew Kapil feeling for her.

'OK friends, thanks to all of you for making my day special.' Soon, Shalu was surrounded by all and everyone personally wished her. Kapil put a sweet in her mouth.

Everything seemed to be normal again.

SEVENTEEN

One year later.

'Yes…yes, you have done it,' Shalu spoke and clenched her fists with joy. A small party was at its culmination in a known restaurant of Kanpur. There were almost six friends in the restaurant and they were gathered to celebrate their new innings of class eleventh. But, bigger reason was selection of Nitin in Ranji Trophy team of Uttar Pradesh and he was the centre of attraction amongst all his friends.

'Yes, look at the headlines, "Nitin broke Jatin's record of Ranji Trophy", Vishal said, putting the leading English daily on the table.

'I am very proud of you, Nitin. After all you delivered what you told us.' Shalu looked into his eyes.

'It's just the beginning. I have miles-way to go,' Nitin said.

'It's too big an achievement in itself, Nitin. Jatin played his first Ranji Trophy match at the age of fifteen years and two hundred and thirty two days. But, you will play before reaching that age,' Vishal said.

'Fifteen years and one hundred and eighty nine days will be completed the day U.P. plays the first match of this session against the railways,' Nitin said.

'Fantastic achievement, 'Shalu got up and gave a light kiss on Nitin's cheek. As usual her act turned Kapil's face red.

'Now, friends, Nitin will break Jatin's next record of making a century in the Ranji debut match,' Kapil made a satire on him. He was seated next to Nitin.

'Why can't he? He is capable of doing that!' Shalu gave a reply even before Nitin could open his mouth. The waiter intervened and started serving the food.

'Why are you so silent Nitin?' Kapil asked.

'Nothing, I was just thinking about the practice. I will have to spend more hours in the net as only fifteen days are left for the match.' Nitin replied.

'You are already batting five hours daily. If you increase the limit, then it might affect your health.' Kapil remarked.

'Kapil is absolutely right,' Shalu said.

'Yesterday, the Srivastava Society Association announced a prize of one lakh rupees for his achievement,' Kapil said.

'Yes, the chairman called up papa and informed him,' Nitin said.

'Wow! What a great news it is!' Shalu started clapping.

'But, how did you know this?' Nitin asked.

'This news was published in today's newspaper.' Kapil got up saying that.

'Hey, where are you going?' Nitin asked. Kapil lifted his index finger up and walked towards the washroom. In between, he met a waiter, who was well acquainted with Kapil as Kapil was almost a weekly visitor in that restaurant. Kapil asked about his well being, gave him a hundred rupees, and returned to his seat.

'You took so long,' Shalu said.

'Actually, I came across an acquaintance on the first floor,' Kapil replied.

OK, come guys, let's have lunch.' Kapil started putting the plates before his friends.

'Kapil Tiwari, today you seem to be in a jolly mood.' Shalu said.

'Obviously, it's the celebration of my brother's victory,' Kapil replied.

His friends became busy in having lunch and the burst of laughters continued along with it. As the lunch got over, the waiter came with a jug of water. Kapil lifted the jug and started pouring water into his glass. He, deliberately, dropped the water down on Nitin's of left palm. As the water touched Nitin's hand, he cried loudly.

'Oh shit, *mummy...mummy...*' This took attention of those people also, who were seated even far.

'What happened?' Shalu asked.

'My hand has got burnt. The water was very hot.' Within a minute there were ulcers on Nitin's palm and the upper hand.

'Who is the bastard who brought the water? Manager, Manager,' Shalu cried out loudly.

'We will see the manager later. I am taking Nitin to a doctor,' Vishal said.

'You are right.' After few minutes, Vishal took Nitin along with him on his bike.

'Hey, who is the bastard who brought this jug?' Kapil pretended.

'Did you bring it?' he asked a twenty year old boy.

'Yes, sir,' the waiter also pretended.

'Are you mad or blind?'

'Sorry, sir, it was my mistake.'

'Call your manager here, I will kick you out,' Kapil pretended to be angry.

'Sorry sir, I am sorry,' the waiter fell down at Kapil's feet. While continuing the drama.

'Leave him, Kapil, we should move now. Nitin will not get alright by kicking him out,' Shalu told.

'Just get out of here,' Kapil acted again. After making the payment, both left the restaurant.

'Hey, how will you go back home?' Kapil asked Shalu as they stepped outside.

'I will go by bus,' Shalu replied.

'Why will you go by bus? What will happen to my new Honda City then?' Kapil said looking excited.

'Where is it?' Shalu asked.

'Look at that last one,' Kapil signaled.

'Wow! It is beautiful, but why didn't you tell everyone?' Shalu asked.

'Actually, I wanted to show you first.' Kapil replied.

'Hmmm, Congratulations.' Shalu said by shaking hand.

'Papa gave me as a gift hardly a week back. He had promised that if I get more than eighty per cent marks, he will gift me a Honda City,' Kapil said.

'Oh! Very nice. By the way, how will you take me? You are a minor. What will happen if the police stops us?' Shalu said sporting worry on her face.

'No one has the courage in the entire Kanpur city to stop the car of Dharmendra Tiwari's son,' Kapil uttered with pride.

'Oh! Really,' Shalu remarked.

'Yes, I have come driving myself.' 'It's OK,' You don't have to worry. Come, sit and admire my car.' Kapil made way for her. His act brought a smile on her face. Shalu sat in the front seat of the car and Kapil was very happy as he executed his plan successfully.

'Whom are you calling?' Kapil asked as he saw Shalu pressing the buttons of her mobile.

'Nitin would be in so much pain.' Shalu's reply took shine off Kapil's face.

'Nitin, are you OK?' Shalu asked Nitin on phone.

'Yes, I am OK. Doctor has wrapped up the bandage. I won't be able to bat at least for four to five days. There is a lot of swelling on the upper portion of palm, and the skin has got burnt, too,' Nitin spoke through his mobile.

'By the way, how will you go back home?' Nitin asked on phone.

'Don't worry. Kapil will drop me home in his new Honda City,' Shalu replied.

'New Honda City.' (voice came through Nitin's mobile)

'Yes, he got a gift from his father.' Shalu replied.

'But, he didn't tell us. He must have borne all the expense of the party, no?' 'By the way, congratulate him on my behalf and take care. Bye. See you tomorrow, and love you.'

'Love you too.' Shalu's last line left Kapil's throat almost dry.

'Is the chat over?' Kapil asked.

'Yes, by the way, your car is fantastic.' Shalu complimented.

'It was not till five minutes back. Now, it has become many times beautiful,' Kapil replied.

'How,' Shalu asked in surprise.

'Because of you,' Kapil spoke fondly.

'I think you should move the car ahead,' Shalu changed the topic.

'Yes, you are right.' The car started moving fast.

'Kapil Tiwari, today you must have borne the expenses of the party as you got the new car,' Shalu asked.

'Yes, I will throw another party also, soon. It can be done within five minutes for you,' Kapil replied.

'How?' Shalu looked at him in surprise.

'It will be at my place. We will reach in five minutes,' Kapil said.

'No, I have to reach home as early as possible.'

'Please, Shalu, I have requested you more than ten times,' Kapil sported despondence on his face.

'OK, but not more than fifteen minutes,' Shalu agreed.

'OK,' he said with a smile on his face.

Kapil then drove away the car to his house.

* * *

'Wow! What a beautiful house!' Shalu said as she stepped out of the car.

'Is this your house?' Shalu kept looking at the house with surprise.

'Yes,' Kapil smiled.

'I have passed by this house more than hundred times. I did not know that you live in this house,' told Shalu.

'How you could know as you never asked my address,' Kapil said.

'Honestly, Kapil, this is my dream house. I always had dream of owning such a grand house. Believe me, whenever I passed by this house with my friends, I used to tell them the same.' Shalu words stretched the smile on Kapil's face by two inches.

'Will you keep praising or come inside?' Kapil remarked.

'Oh! Sorry, I forgot.' Shalu and Kapil started walking towards the gate Shalu as still overwhelmed.

'*Kaka*, please open the gate,' Kapil told the guard standing at the gate of his house.

'OK, Kappu *baba*,' a well dressed man in his fifties came out of a small wooden room and opened the gate.

'Wow! What a fantastic swimming pool. It is so big.' Shalu was completely lost in the pool. The bungalow was huge and built on a in huge plot. As Shalu, along with Kapil, was walking towards the house, different words came out of her mouth, 'Wow! It looks as if it is heaven, what a beautiful carving through the marble.' With each word, proud and shine increased on Kapil's face.

After walking for almost two hundred metres, both entered the bungalow. Kapil took Shalu to the first floor and said, 'This is my room, Shalu.'

'Very beautiful,' Shalu observed the costly paintings and carpet.

By the way, what will you have? Anything cold or hot?' Kapil asked.

'Something cold,' Shalu replied. Kapil picked up the cordless phone and gave the order in a low tone.

'I have separate study and sports room as well,' Kapil bragged.

'Sports room,' Shalu raised her eyebrows.

'Yes, sports room, where I keep my kit-bags and other stuff,' Kapil told.

Suddenly a well dressed servant, with two colleagues, entered the room.

“Here your order” Kapil signaled. All the servants swung into action and started the proceeding. Within minutes, a variety of food and snacks were laid in front of Shalu. She was surprised to see almost ten types of juice, dry fruits and, various type of sweets as well.

‘Have you gone mad?’ Shalu said.

‘Why?’

‘There are only two of us in the room, not twenty,’ Shalu reprimanded him.

‘I know, dear. You can choose whatever you want to eat,’ Kapil replied softly.

‘I should complain to aunty about you. Where she is?’ Shalu remarked.

‘She has gone to my aunt’s house in Dehradun,’ Kapil said.

‘And your father,’ Shalu continued to speak.

‘He is in Australia for a business deal and will come after three days,’ Kapil replied.

‘Do you live alone in such a big house?’ Shalu stopped drinking juice and asked with surprise.

‘Yes, what’s the problem?’ Kapil spoke casually.

‘I mean, you don’t feel afraid living alone in such a huge bungalow,’ Shalu expressed.

‘Am I alone?There is a staff of almost fifty people. My friends and cousins keep visiting almost every day,’ Kapil assured Shalu.

‘What kind of business is your father running?’ Shalu asked.

‘We have leather, chemical and cement factories,’ Kapil replied.

‘Wow! Everything is yours as you don’t have a brother or sister,’ Shalu spoke in excitement.

‘It’s obvious, but I have a different goal,’ Kapil replied in a somber tone.

‘What?’

‘I have to play for India. It’s my father’s biggest dream.’ Kapil took a long breath after saying that.

'Ohhh,'

'By the way, how do you feel in my house, Shalu?' Kapil changed the topic.

'Really, it's very nice. Now, I will have to come here regularly.' Shalu smiled.

'I want the same,' Kapil said in a very low tone.

'What did you say?' she was startled.

'Nothing, I said it's very good that you like my house,' Kapil said.

'I told you earlier that it's my dream house. I hope one day, Nitin and I would live together in this type of house,' Shalu spoke emotionally.

'But, how is it possible?'

It's very much possible. One day he would be a star cricketer of India,' Shalu spoke with pride.

'If that doesn't come true then what will you do?' Kapil's question brought a wave of seriousness on Shalu's face.

'I have full confidence in Nitin's ability and God,' replied Shalu after thinking for a while.

'Just think about it. If Nitin didn't become a star, then?'

'Let's see what happens. Whatever happens, I will face that.' Shalu released a long breath.

'Hmmm! By the way, you need not worry. If Nitin didn't become a big star, then my house is always open for you,' Kapil remarked.

'What did you say?' Shalu stopped drinking the juice.

'Nothing, I am just kidding,' Kapil smiled.

'By the way, what does your father do?' Kapil asked Shalu.

'He is running a business of medicines but, not as big as your father is.'

'It will not create any problem in our relationship,' Kapil tried to give the message to her again.

'What relationship?' Shalu asked.

'Nothing,' Kapil replied.

'Kapil Tiwari, I should make a move now. It has been forty five minutes while I promised you fifteen minutes,' Shalu said casting a gaze on her wrist watch.

'When will you come next?' Kapil asked in hope.

'Let's see,' Shalu replied.

'Should I drop you to your house?' Kapil offered.

'Thanks, no need to take that trouble,' Shalu denied.

'Bye Kapil and thanks a lot for the hospitality,'

'You are embarrassing me. I didn't do anything,'

'Bye,'

'Let me drop you to the gate,'

Yes, why not,' Shalu smiled. Both of them started walking towards the gate of the bungalow.

EIGHTEEN

Next Day

10 a.m.

Nitin was talking to Vishal in a park in front of his house.

'I am fed up now. It's been four days since I practiced,' Nitin said.

'It's a matter of few days. Your injury will heal completely in two-three days,' Vishal said while inspecting Nitin's palm closely by taking in his hand.

'You can understand how tough it is to pass time these days. All the players are busy practicing and I am sitting frustrated in my house,' Nitin spoke feeling helpless.

'Don't worry. Everything will be fine.' Vishal told.

'Vishal, I have to tell you something,' Nitin pondered.

'What?'

'I have to meet God,'

'Meaning, Jatin Tendulkar,'

'Yes,'

'But, why?'

'I wished that if I get selected, I will go to meet him to seek his blessings,'

'No problem, but will he meet you?'

'If we try, we can meet him,' Nitin said.

'But…!'

'I have a friend who plays for Mumbai under-sixteen team. I have taken the details from him. As you know that Jatin is injured and taking rest at home these days, it would be easy to meet him.' Nitin said.

'But, we will have to pay at least five thousand rupees for two people.' Vishal said.

'Hmmmm, I have around two thousand,' Nitin replied.

'And I also have the same amount,' Vishal said.

'It means that we are short by one thousand rupees,' Nitin said with a worried face.

'Why are you so disappointed? You should ask for it from Shalu. She will give you double the amount,' Vishal suggested.

'Are you foolish? She has already helped me a lot. More so, I don't want anyone to know that we are going to Mumbai to meet Jatin.' Nitin spoke.

'I think, four thousand rupees would be enough,' Nitin spoke again.

'What will happen, in case of emergency, or we have to stay over there for one or two days more?' Vishal expressed concern.

'*Mom* saves money in her piggy bank every day and it is kept in her makeshift temple.' Nitin looked into Vishal's eyes.

'Hmmm, take some money out of the piggy bank. Aunty will never come to know about this. Put the money back again whenever you get a prize in a tournament.' Vishal told Nitin.

'You are absolutely right.' Nitin had twinkle in his eyes.

'You book two tickets for Mumbai,' Nitin told Vishal.

'But, what will you say to uncle and aunty?' Vishal asked Nitin.

'I will tell mom that I have to go to Delhi to take the match fee, which I played last month,' Nitin thought and replied.

'Yes, that's a good idea.' Vishal confirmed.

NINETEEN

Five days later.

'Hey, brother, is there any budget hotel around?' Nitin asked a taxi driver Kishan Dharekar, outside Victoria Terminus station.

'Yes, there are so many,' replied the driver who was in his forties.

'What will be the charge?' Both asked.

'It should be around five hundred rupees per day,' the driver replied without even looking at them.

'By the way, how far away is Jatin Tendulkar's house from here?' the driver took a break from cleaning his car and stared at both of them for almost half a minute.

'Where do you have to go, hotel or Tendalya's house?' the driver became soft in his words.

'First, we will go to the hotel and then, to your Tendalya's house.' Vishal's reply brought a smile on driver's face.

'It means that you will stay in that hotel, which is nearby Tendalya's house,' the driver looked curious.

'Yes, you are right uncle,' Vishal said.

'But, the hotels near Tendalya's house are bit expensive.'

'What would be the charge for one day?'

'At least five thousand rupees,'

'Uncle, please take us to that hotel, which is as close as possible and fits in our budget, too,' Vishal intervened.

'Hmmm, let me think.'

'Since you have come to meet Tendalya, I will help you,' the driver said.

'Would you like to stay in a room instead of hotel?' the driver asked after thinking for a few seconds.

'What's the advantage for us ?'

'Actually, my fellow driver has gone to Bihar for few days. He has given the keys to me. Tendalya's house is around thirty kilometres from that room. It would be suitable for you,' the driver said.

'How much will you charge us for that?' Nitin asked.

'One thousand rupees for each person and five hundred extra for pick up and drop from Tendalya's house,' the driver replied.

'Uncle, it's too much. Please give us some concession,' Vihal requested.

'My son, if you stay in any hotel, you will have to pay minimum two to three thousand. I have given you a very good deal,' the driver replied.

'Please, uncle,' Nitin requested.

'OK, I will give you a discount of five hundred rupees in rent, but nothing less than that,' the driver said.

'OK, uncle, this is done.' Both sat in the taxi, and within minutes, the taxi was rolling.

'Hey, this room is very messy,' Nitin said as the driver, Kishan Dharekar, opened the room. It was a small single room in a very old apartment. The room was entirely scraggy and things, like clothes, were scattered and unwashed pots were lying on the floor. Moreover, it was stinking.

'Oh! It would be tough for us to live here,' Vishal said.

'You will not get a five-star room in fifteen hundred rupees,' the driver remarked.

'Do you want to stay here or shall I go?' the driver asked with perkiness.

'It's OK', Nitin and Vishal gave consent to each other through their eyes.

'Very good, you made a good decision. By the way, please give fifteen hundred rupees in advance and tell me what time should I come in the evening?' the driver spoke.

'How much time will it take to reach Tendalya's house?' Vishal asked while handing over the money to him.

'At least two hours.'

'Two hours!' Both, Nitin and Vishal, sounded simultaneously in surprise.

'Yes, because of the traffic jam, even thirty kilometers will be covered in almost two hours. It's Mumbai, not your Kanpur.'

'Hmmm, then you must come around 6:00 p.m.

'It's OK, and you can eat just outside the building. Food is available at very low and affordable price,' the driver suggested.

'OK, thanks.' As the driver left the room, both of them first started to put the things in order and then slept on the small bed after almost fifteen minutes.

* * *

'Oh! Shit!' Nitin said, punching his right fist on the palm of his left hand. Around 6:20 p.m., Vishal and Nitin were sitting in Kishan Dharekar's taxi.

'Now, what happened? Have you forgotten something?' Kishan asked while driving.

'Come on, we didn't take any gift for Tendalya.' Nitin said.

'Oh! I forgot, too,' Vishal said with a bit of sadness in his voice.

'What can be done, now?' Nitin thought loudly.

'I think we should purchase a pack of dry fruits.' Vishal suggested.

'That's a good idea,' Kishan responded to Nitin's suggestion.

'Uncle, please stop the car in front of a known shop.' Nitin requested Kishan.

'Don't worry, son.' After almost ten minutes, they purchased two kilos of sweets.

'My son, your wait is over. Tendalya's house is very close,' Kishan Dharekar put pressure on the paddle.

'Where, where?' both spoke from the back seat.

'Look at that wide road. At the end of this road, you will find the colony. On the wall you will find these words written in bold letters:

"Krishna Niwas. Tendalya lives in the same colony".' The driver, Kishan Dharekar replied.

'Will we be allowed to go inside?' Nitin asked.

'Well, that's your problem how you manage to get inside. Let me go now. Shall I come at 11 o'clock?' Kishan asked.

'Yes,' Nitin replied. Soon, Kishan became invisible from there along with his taxi.

* * *

'Hey, who are you and where are you going?' A watchman, around forty five, swiftly came out of the small room shouting, just outside the gate, as he saw both, Nitin and Vishal, trying to enter the colony, Krishna Niwas.

'We have come from Kanpur and we want to meet Tendalya,' Nitin said.

'Do you know him? Have you taken an appointment?' the watchman asked, sporting a big moustache, and a rifle was hanging on his right shoulder.

'I am the biggest fan of Tendalya,' Vishal said.

'Me, too,' Nitin said even before the watchman spoke.

'Everybody says the same thing. Hundreds of people come here daily and claim the same. Does it mean that Tendalya should meet everyone?' the watchman asked.

'We have come from Kanpur,' Nitin said.

'People come here even from London. Just go away.'

'No, 'we won't. We will go only after meeting Tendalya,' Vishal said.

'You can't even put your feet inside till I am here.' Hearing the argument, a few onlookers gathered around them.

'Uncle, actually, I am Nitin Srivastava. I am the same boy, who will break Tendalya's record just next month by playing in Ranji Trophy,' Nitin tried to convince the watchman by showing cutting from an English newspaper.

'You will not be allowed to go inside even if you are Bradman.'

'What happened Shiva?' An onlooker intervened.

'Good evening Ajit sir. These boys were trying to enter the colony. They want to meet Jatin Sir.'

'Hey boys, is this true?' That guy, around fifty, said.

'Yes, sir. We are huge fans of him and have come from Kanpur, especially to meet him.' Nitin answered.

'It's not easy to meet him, my son. Thousands of people come to meet him. It is not possible for him to make each and every person happy.' The gentleman explained.

'Sir,'

'Sorry, dear, I can't help you.' That man left the place.

'Come what may, we will not return without meeting with him,' Nitin said.

'Uncle, just do one thing. Call Tendalya and inform him. We will do whatever he says,' Nitin said beseechingly.

'OK, I will try. But, first you stand outside the gate. I will inform you within fifteen minutes,' the watchman assured.

'We will wait,' both came out of that wide road, which ended at the starting point of Krishna Niwas.

TWENTY

'Hello, sir, I am Shiva speaking. Two young boys have come from Kanpur and want to meet you,' the watchman spoke through the phone, which was inside a small guardroom.

'No, Shiva, it's not possible for me at this time. It's almost 9:00 p.m.,' Jatin replied.

'Sir, they have come from Kanpur and have been here for more than an hour.'

'Shiva, I have high temperature. Make them understand with love and affection, OK,' Jatin said.

'OK, sir, Good night,'

'Good night, Shiva.'

'What did he say?' Nitin rushed to the watchman, desperately, as he saw him coming.

'Actually, Tendalya has got high fever. I got this information from his elder brother,' the watchman replied.

'Hmmm,' Nitin and Vishal sported sadness on their faces.

'OK, uncle, thanks.' Both said.

'Either he got the wrong information or he was lying,' Vishal said.

'What do you mean?' Nitin asked.

'The watchman was telling a lie. Didn't you notice his tone and expressions?' Vishal said.

'You are right,' Nitin said.

'If we want to meet Jatin, then we will have to do something special,' Nitin said.

'What special?' Vishal became more attentive.

'We will spend the whole night here.' Nitin said.

'What!'

'Yes,'

'When early in the morning Jatin comes to know about this, he will, for sure, come to meet us. Even if he goes elsewhere, he will pass in front of us and then, we will talk to him,' Nitin said.

'But, we can come tomorrow as well,' Vishal spoke.

'No, we have very less money to stay in Mumbai. We will have to play master stroke. Now whatever happens, will happen tomorrow.' Nitin remarked.

'Have you gone mad? You will spend the whole night in cold,' Kishan Dharekar, who had come in between, scolded them.

'We will not die, uncle.' Nitin said.

'But, this is madness my son.' Kishan replied.

'You can say anything, uncle. Please go now. We will wait till the morning.' Nitin argued.

'As you wish, I can only make you understand. By the way, at what time should I come in the morning?' Kishan gave up on them.

'Around 10 o'clock,' Nitin replied.

Kishan Dharekar left the place. Within ten minutes, it was going to be 11 p.m. The crowd had begun to disperse.

'As the night progresses, it will chilly,' Vishal said while rubbing his palms with each other.

'We will have to find a way.' Nitin said.

'Look at this,' Nitin pointed out towards a makeshift ironing shop.

'What is that?' Vishal asked.

'I think, you must not put pressure on your mind to understand that,' Nitin replied.

'I know that this is an ironing shop, then?' Vishal asked.

'We will sleep here.' Nitin suggested.

'Hmmm, that's good. We haven't got any option either,' Vishal smiled.

'These days will be remembered forever,' Nitin said and took out a sheet from his handbag.

'Yes, will be remembered forever.' Vishal repeated what Nitin spoke.

'Hey, sheet in your handbag! Had you already planned this in your mind?' Vishal asked.

'No, it's a coincidence that I didn't notice the sheet and it remained in my bag.' Nitin replied.

'It's only one, and we are two,' Nitin smiled.

'Have you forgotten the time when four of us slept in one sheet?' Vishal remarked.

'I have all the things in my mind.' Both kept talking till late in the night and then slept off.

* * *

'Hey, get up who is sleeping here? Hey, you both are still here!' the watchman, Shiva, spoke with surprise as he stretched the sheet. It was around 6:30 a.m.

'Yes,' both got up yawning.

'It's strange that you spent the whole night here!' Shiva said.

'What else could we do?' Nitin said.

'After all, what do you want?' Shiva asked folding both his hands.

'A meeting with Tendalya.' Nitin replied.

'Oh God! Now I will have to do something,' Shiva spoke softly.

'OK, freshen up first and have breakfast. If you walk straight for around two hundred metres, you will find a public toilet. Come back at 10:00 a.m.', Shiva said.

'OK,' Vishal and Nitin started to walk straight.

'Good morning, sir,' Shiva called through phone.

'Good morning, Shiva. How are you?' Jatin replied.

'Sir, a strange situation has come up,' Shiva told Jatin.

'What happened?' Jatin asked.

'Sir, those boys spent the whole night at Raju's shop.' Shiva apprised Jatin.

'Which boys are you talking about?' Jatin asked.

'Sir, those boys, who came to meet you yesterday, from Kanpur.' Shiva spoke.

'What! Are they mad?' Jatin shouted.

'Sir, please meet them. They are mad for you.' Shiva requested.

'OK, ask them to come around 10 o'clock, at the gate of the colony. Make sure that media does not get any hint about this.' Jatin warned.

'You need not worry, sir.' Shiva assured.

TWENTY ONE

'Hey, Jatin sir,' both Nitin and Vishal, rushed towards Jatin as they saw him at the gate. Jatin was in a black tracksuit.

'It's unbelievable,' both touched his feet and kept looking at him, absolutely stunned.

Suddenly, Nitin embraced with Jatin and was in tears. Even Jatin didn't try to take himself off. Nitin was almost crying.

'Hey, why are you crying my boy?' Jatin rubbed his hand on his head.

'Sir, he is crying because of happiness', Vishal said this time. Niting kept embracing to him almost for a minute.

'How are you?' Jatin asked politely.

'Sir, nice,' both replied.

'Why did you sleep out in cold? It was wrong,' Jatin spoke. Both kept quiet.

'Sir, I am sorry. But I have come for a specific purpose.' Nitin said.

'What purpose?' Jatin asked.

'Sir, I wanted to take your blessings. I have been selected in U.P. Ranji Trophy team. Next month, I will become the youngest Indian to play the Ranji match.' Nitin replied.

'Are you Nitin Srivastava?' Jatin asked.

'Yes sir, but how did you know?' Nitin was overwhelmed.

'Some of my friends mentioned about you. Even I read the newspaper.' Jatin spoke.

'Thanks, sir, it's an honour for me.' Nitin replied.

'Sir, we have brought a small gift for you,' Vishal said.

'What?'

'Sir, it a token of love from us.' Vishal forwarded a pack of sweets and Nitin also extended his hand to touch the box.

Oh! Thank you very much. Jatin said, it's a famous shop of Mumbai. I have been eating sweets of this shop from my childhood days,' Jatin said as he saw the confectioner's name was printed on packet and he kept talking to both of them for fifteen minutes.

'OK, Nitin and Vishal, it was nice meeting you,' Jatin sought permission to go.

'Thanks a lot, sir. I will remember this meeting forever. Sir, give your blessings, so that I could score well in my debut Ranji match, like you.' Nitin touched Jatin's feet, again.

'My blessings are always with you. May your dreams come true!' Jatin hugged both of them one by one and went inside. Both kept looking at Jatin till he became invisible completely.

'Thank you very much uncle. It happened only because of you,' Nitin said to Shiva.

'And this is a small gift for you as well,' Vishal forwarded a note of five hundred rupees to him.

'Hey, you need not do this. Good thing is that you were able to meet Jatin sir. Let me tell you that you really are blessed and fortunate. I have been working here for more than ten years and Tendalya has never met anyone in such a way,' Shiva said while pushing Vishal's hand back.

'Really, we have been blessed. Thank you very much, uncle.' Nitin said.

'Hey, Kishan uncle has also come.' Vishal pointed out towards the taxi.

'OK uncle, bye-bye. God bless we will meet again.' Both spoke to Kishan.

'Bye, my son.'

Both rushed towards the finishing point of the road.

'Did you meet Tendalya?' Kishan asked.

'Yes, and talked to him for almost half an hour.'

'Really?' He looked at them with surprise.

'Yes,'

'And, I have also played a part in this,' Kishan said.

'Why not uncle, you too have played your part. Thank you very much.'

'I am just kidding. Sit in the taxi and take rest for a few hours as you have to catch the train at night.' Both took the seat and taxi started moving towards its destination.

'Thank you very much uncle,' Vishal said getting down from the taxi at the railway station in Mumbai at around 9:00 p.m.

'This is a small gift for you from our side,' Nitin took out a packet of sweets from his handbag and gave to Kishan Dharekar.

'Hey, there was no need of this,' Kishan said.' Had you not helped us, it would have been impossible for us to meet Tendalya?' Vishal said.

'Yes, it's very much true as we did not have enough money to stay in Mumbai. You helped us with an accommodation. Thank you very much again.' Nitin said.

'Thank you, my son, may God fulfill your all dreams,' Kishan hugged both of them simultaneously with tears in his eyes.

'At what time will your train come?' Kishan asked.

'11:00 p.m.,' Vishal said.

'Have you purchased the ticket?' Kishan asked.

'Vishal has already arranged the tickets on phone this morning. One of his father's friend is a senior officer in railways.' Nitin replied.

'OK, son, let me do my job. A customer is calling,' Kishan Dharekar said as someone called, 'Taxi, taxi.' After few minutes, as Dharekar went away in his taxi, Nitin and Vishal entered the railway station.

Around 9:30 p.m.

Both were waiting for the train, sitting on a bench. Suddenly, Nitin got up and started walking. 'Vishal, you sit here, I'll come back in five minutes,' Nitin said.

'Where are you going?' Vishal asked.

'I am going to a book stall. I have to purchase the recent edition a magzine which is on Jatin.'

'OK.'

'Hey, Vishal, Vishal,' after ten minutes, Nitin came running to Vishal. He seemed to be very nervous and tears were rolling down his cheek.

'What happened, why are you crying?' Vishal asked.

'My purse is stolen.' Nitin replied.

'What! Where did you keep it?' Vishal looked worried.

'It was in the back pocket of my trouser,' Nitin replied, weeping.

'Oh shit! Why did you keep it in the back pocket? I have told you a number of times, but you always follow your own mind.' Vishal reprimanded Nitin.

'By the way, what was there in the purse?' Vishal asked.

'Tickets, and seven hundred rupees.' Nitin replied.

'What! You had put the tickets in the purse,' Vishal sat on his knees and held his head.

'Oh God! What will happen now? I have only three hundred and twenty rupees,' Vishal stood up after two minutes.

'Now, what will happen Vishal? Shall I call Kishan uncle?' Nitin asked.

'No,' Vishal spoke sternly.

'Then, what?' Nitin asked.

'What? One of us will have to travel without ticket,' Vishal said.

'But, it's not a matter of going from Kanpur to Lucknow. It will take almost two days to reach Kanpur,' Nitin said in a weepy voice.

'Now, whatever happens, we will face it. But, will not give more trouble to Kishan uncle,' Vishal reiterated.

* * *

'Everyone is sleeping. Spread the sheet under the seat and lay down silently under the lower berth,' Vishal said at around 12:20 a.m. Nitin followed his instructions immediately. He got down from the upper birth and lay under the lower birth.

'Make sure that no part of the sheet comes out of the seat,' Vishal said. Soon, both were snoring. In the night, around 3 a.m., T. T. E. (Train ticket examiner) came for inspection of the ticket, but he didn't cast even an iota of doubt that someone was sleeping under the bench.

* * *

'Hey, who is hiding here?' Around 6:00 a.m., Nitin got the attention of a passenger, who was reading the newspaper.

'Yes, who is hiding? Come out.' In between, Vishal almost jumped off the upper berth. All the passengers, who were sitting around, started to look under the berth.

'Yes, uncle, this is my brother,' Vishal intervened.

It's OK. But why is he hiding under the lower berth?' A guy, in his fifties, asked.

'Uncle, actually, his purse was stolen at the station. Since we lost all the money and ticket as well, that's why we applied this tactic.' Vishal explained.

'Oh! Don't worry my, son. The T.T.E. will not touch him till I am here. Come out of the berth, son.' one old guy said.

'Yes, come out,' few voices sounded simultaneously. Nitin came out.

'*Uffff*! How painful night it must have been for you,' that man showed sympathy to Nitin by saying this to him.

'It was in our destiny, sir. It was bound to happen,' Vishal said.

'By the way, you don't worry. I will see who bothers this young man. The calamity could happen with anyone. If the T.T.E. doesn't agree, then I will pay for his ticket.'

'Why only you will pay, sir? We all will share,' so many sounds brought a smile on both the faces Nitin and Vishal.

TWENTY TWO

Two years later.

'Hey Shalu, please come. Why are you bothering me?' Nitin said gasping, while Shalu was running all around.

'You got tired only in five minutes. I have more stamina than you, my cricketer', Shalu stopped at the finishing point of the stairs and started to run to get down the stairs. It was almost a distance of five metres between both the stairs. This play was going on between both of them for last few minutes in Shalu's house as there was no one else in the house.

'Are you challenging me?' Nitin said.

'Yes, I am challenging you.' Shalu replied.

'Now save yourself, if you can,' Nitin started chasing much faster than before. Shalu, too, was wanting the same from within. She cut down her speed. Nitin caught her from behind and lifted her in his hands.

'Don't challenge me, ever,' Nitin said.

'It's OK, dear,' Shalu kissed on his lips, lying in his lap. Nitin responded with the same kind of love. Nitin took her into a room and lay her down. He, then, sat on the bed and both were completely lost in each others' eyes.

'You are looking beautiful,' Nitin said.

'Really?' Shalu asked.

'Really,' Nitin started kissing on her lips passionately. Shalu, too, was giving the same response. She had worn a black mini-skirt and a red top. The cuddling and rolling in bed went on for almost fifteen minutes.

'I will be far away from you for almost one month, for the first time,' Nitin said, staring at the roof. He lay down on the bed just next to Shalu.

'I will miss you a lot,' Shalu caught his hand and kissed on the back of his palm.

'This is an important Ranji Trophy session for you. In the debut, you were not up to the expectations, and in the last session, you missed all the matches because of your injury.' Shalu said.

'I know, dear, I know very well that I have failed to do what Jatin did in his early days.' Nitin replied.

'Why do you always compare yourself with Jatin,' Shalu spoke in irritation.

'I am not comparing. I am just saying my part.' Nitin spoke.

'No, you more often than not, seemed to be comparing yourself with Jatin.' Shalu reiterated.

'You are getting me wrong, Shalu.'

'No, I am talking in the right way. If you talk to any person, he will understand the same,' Shalu replied.

'OK, I will not do it now,' Nitin said.

'You should set your own target Nitin?' Shalu said.

'I have already set my target.' Nitin spoke.

'What?'

'Under-nineteen World Cup. It will take place after two years, in Bangladesh. It's going to be a big platform for me. If we win and I become the highest run scorer, it would be easy for me to enter into the Indian team,' Nitin said. 'Is it so important?' Shalu asked.

'Look at Mohammad Kaif and Yuvraj Singh. They joined the Indian team in less than a year of playing under-nineteen World Cup,' Nitin spoke.

'Hmmm, it's still two years to go for the World Cup. Focus on Ranji Trophy matches.' Shalu said.

'It's OK, dear,' Nitin turned towards his right and kissed on Shalu's lips.

'I have to tell you one important thing,' Nitin said.

'Tell,' Shalu said.

'You already know that after twenty days, Reena *di*'s marriage will take place.'

'Then,'

'What, then? On that day I will either be batting or fielding against Madhya Pradesh in Indore. It will be the second day of the match,' Nitin said.

'You have to reach my house early in the morning and look after Reena *di*. In the evening, you will give me the details.' Nitin requested Shalu.

'No need to worry about it,' this time Shalu turned her left side and started to suck his lips.

'By the way, what are you giving to your sister as her wedding gift?' Shalu asked.

'First promise me that you will not disclose it to anyone.' Nitin said.

'Promise,' Shalu replied.

'One lakh rupees,' Nitin said.

'One lakh rupees! Where did you get them from?' Shalu came into a sitting position.

'Almost two years back, Kanpur *Srivastava* (a caste in India) *Samaj Samiti* (a social group) had honoured me and gave me fifty thousand cash.' Nitin spoke.

'But, for what?' Shalu was curious.

'Come on, you forgot. They gave it to me for breaking Jatin's record and being the youngest player ever to play the Ranji Trophy match,' Nitin tried to remind her.

'Yes, I remember very well,' Shalu said.

'I had purchased gold with that amount. The price is almost double now, I mean, around one lakh and thirty thousand rupees.

'Great! I really love you Nitin.' This time Shalu sat on Nitin's stomach and started sucking his lips again, and kept doing it for next few minutes.

'I love you too, Shalu.'

TWENTY THREE

Twenty days later

Nitin's house was twittering as the preparations of Reena's marriage were in full swing. Guests were everywhere. Some people were busy in the park, chatting in groups. Some were keeping an eye on foot arrangement. Children were left to themselves and the following song was echoing loudly, "*Bachke too rehna re bachke too rehna, nahi tujhko mauka milega sambhalna...*" (a song from a hit bollywood movie, Company).

'Where have you put the garland? I have been searching it for more than an hour now,' Savitri said as she saw Seetaram, her husband.

'I have yet to bring the garland,' he replied.

'But, just one hour back you told me that you have brought it,' Savitri said.

'I think your ears are buzzing. Why are you so nervous?' Seetaram said.

'Who will not be nervous on her only daughter's marriage? Are you not?' Savitri asked.

'I am feeling relieved than nervous.' Seetaram replied.

'Just go and bring the garland along with ten pieces of betel and a small pack of vermillion,' Savitri pointed to Seetaram.

'OK,' Seetaram said and left the house.

'Brother, put the flotilla properly. Has Reena come or not?' Giving instructions to a man, who was busy in decorations, Savitri threw a question at her younger sister. Savitri was leading from the front and kept an eye on the preparations.

'No, I gave a call at the beauty parlour and got a reply that Reena will take at least one hour more,' Savitri's sister replied.

'Shalu, have you checked her dress properly?' Savitri asked.

Don't worry, aunty. I have put her dress and jewellery in a big case.' Shalu assured.

'That's good. Remind me if there is any other work left to be done. It is 11:30 a.m. and the marriage procession will come at around 3:00 p.m.' Time kept passing like that and everyone became attentive when the famous band's voice touched everyone's ears. Activities paced up in the house and the noise became louder than earlier.

* * *

'Hey, Reena *di*, why are you looking so dejected?' Shalu asked.

'Shalu, I have only one brother and he is not with me on this day of my life.' Tears started rolling down her cheeks.

'Don't be sad, Reena. After all, he is playing to fulfill everyone's dream,' Savitri turned up to her as she heard them talking.

'Aunty is absolutely right, Reena *di*,' Shalu said.

I know that Shalu. But, this day will never come again. I am missing him a lot,' Reena said.

'We, too, are missing him a lot. But don't shed tears, otherwise, you will start looking like a witch.' As Savitri said this, the room echoed with loud bursts of laughter, and it brought a smile on Shalu's face.

'Take this and wipe your tears, otherwise, it will affect your make-up,' Shalu gave a napkin to Reena.

'Hey, how are you Gupta ji? You are most welcome, sir, you are most welcome,' Seetaram repeated the words and rushed to greet Narendra Gupta, who was the father of the groom, Rajesh.

'Sir, you came so early. How long will the marriage procession take to reach?' Seetaram said after hugging him.

'It's about to start. Procession will come soon as it's hardly two kilometers from here,' Mr. Gupta said.

'Come in please, have a seat,' Seetaram said.

'No, I have to return as well. Actually I had come to have some important conversation with you.' Mr. Gupta said.

'Yes, sir, please tell me what can I do?' Seetaram asked politely.

'Will you walk with me a little?' Narendra asked.

'Yes, why not,' Seetaram replied. Both started walking.

'Tell, Gupta *ji*, what were you saying?' Seetaram asked.

'Promise me that you will not mind it,' Mr. Gupta said.

'Why will I mind, sir? Now, we are relatives,' Seetaram hugged him again.

'Actually, I was not willing to tell, but it's Rajesh's will,' Narendra said with hesitation.

'I have no problem, Gupta *ji*. Say with open heart whatever you want to say.' Seetaram spoke.

'The matter is that Rajesh has asked me to tell you to arrange for a bike and one lakh cash', Gupta smiled.

'What!' Seetaram's face turned pale.

'But, sir, I had already told you about my budget,' Seetaram said in a shaky voice.

'You are right Seetaram *ji*. But you know Rajesh got a job only five months back. He has taken loan for his marriage. That's why I......OK, let me go Seetram *ji* as my mobile is buzzing regularly. You have enough time, and consult your relatives too.' Narendra Gupta left the place, but Seetaram was almost in a state of shock. Suddenly, the atmosphere became too heavy for him and he felt darkness around him.

TWENTY FOUR

'What! It's not less than a blackmail,' Savitri was crying. There were only three people in the locked room: Seetaram, Savitri, and Reena.

'Now, what will happen?' Seetaram sat down on the floor and he was in tears.

'Nitin is not here too,' Savitri said.

'Did he use harsh words, or give warning as well?' Savitri put her hand on his shoulder.

'No warning, but he has created a big problem for us. From where will I arrange such a huge amount?' Seetaram was in tears.

'When they are showing such attitude now, they can do anything with my daughter after marriage,' Seetaram ran out of patience and broke down badly.

'It has happened because of me,' Reena also started weeping and she, too, sat down on the floor and hugged her father. Suddenly, Seetaram fell back.

'*Mummy,* see, what has happened to *papa*? His body has become absolutely stiff. Savitri, too, sat down.

'Oh! His body parts seem to freeze,' Savitri started weeping loudly.

'It seems to me that *papa* has suffered a paralysis attack,' both, Reena and Savitri, were weeping loudly. With each passing minute, the marriage procession and music of band were getting louder. As the procession was coming closer to the house, lament and vociferation were taking a new height inside the locked room.

'What happened, aunty? Please open the door,' Vishal was beating the door bitterly. There were ten to eleven people along with him. Soon, Savitri opened the door.

'What happened Savitri?' her younger sister asked.

'Look, what has happened to your brother-in-law. Half side of his body is not working,' Savitri replied, weeping. Seetaram's jaw was distorted. His eyes were not blinking and saliva was coming out of his mouth, slowly.

'Oh God! Uncle has suffered a paralysis attack. We will have to take him to the hospital, immediately,' Vishal said.

'But, the procession is almost at the door,' one relative said.

'Uncle, please close the door before more people enter the room. It is already too suffocation and not good for uncle.' Vishal said.

'Aunty, uncle and I, along with few people, will take Seetaram uncle to the hospital. You can welcome the groom and guests,' Vishal said.

'I will also come with you,' Savitri said.

'But, what will happen here? Who will take care of everyone and, Reena? She needs you. We don't have any other option,' Vishal cried in anger.

'He is absolutely right, Savitri,' Savitri's brother-in-law said.

'Be quick, uncle. Call a rickshaw-puller. And yes, no one will disclose it to the remaining guests and even to Rajesh, OK,' Vishal looked at everyone who were present in the room.

'Don't weep, Reena. Everything will be OK.' Vishal looked towards Reena, who was standing in a corner and weeping continuously.

'We are moving now.' Vishal picked up Seetaram and took him in his lap. Two other people followed him.

'Shalu, you have to be with Reena *di* till the last minute, till she leaves, OK,' Vishal said. Shalu only nodded.

"*Baharon phool barsao mera mehboob aaya hai. . mera mehboob aaya hai*" (a famous Hindi movie song echoed as Reena was heading towards the stage for Jaimala (a tradition of marriage, mainly in northern India. With this tradition, the bride and groom welcome and accept each other by putting garland around each other neck).

'No *di*. Don't cry. People will cast a doubt,' Shalu said to Reena, as a group of girls started moving towards the stage. Reena nodded and tried to sport a fake smile on her face. Reena was crying and there were two pictures running in her mind constantly: one, was the demand set forth by Rajesh's father and second, was the state of her own father. But, along with it, there was one more thought coming to Reena.

Reena covered a distance of almost two hundred metres from the house to stage, which was set in a park. The girls were gyrating, music and dance was on. Finally, she reached the stage. Mockery and laugh was at its best, more from Rajesh's friend. But, all this was making Reena more frustrated and irritated. After a few minutes, the noise stopped. As Rajesh put the garland around Reena's neck, the people gathered around them and clapped but, only to be stunned within minutes. Soon, Reena took her hand up to put the garland around Rajesh's neck. But, instead of that, something else brought the function under a strange silence. A loud sound of slap echoed and Rajesh's cheek turned red by Reena's slap. She broke down loudly. Soon, another slap echoed.

'Why did you do that?' Reena's aunt pushed her in anger.

'I will not marry this man. He and his family have almost killed my father,' Reena started weeping more loudly than earlier.

'What happened, I didn't do anything!' Rajesh said.

'Ask your father. What has he done?' After saying that, Shalu got down from the stage. The remaining people, along with the mother, were trying to convince Reena by taking her off the stage.

'No *mummy*, I will not get married to such a greedy family,' Reena said.

'But, my daughter, our reputation is at stake.' Guests were stunned, some were whispering and waiting for the ceremonies to take place.

'Nothing is left *mummy*. The matter has gone beyond my hands and mind. I can't even think about making this relationship work.

Do you think that they will keep me happy? Do you think his family will ever forget that I slapped him?' Reena said imploringly. Discussion went on for the next few minutes, till Shalu went up to the stage again.

'Let me tell you all that Reena *di* has decided not to marry this man. Almost one hour back, his father demanded one bike and one lakh cash. It is because of this reason that uncle suffered a paralysis attack and is admitted in the hospital,' Shalu spoke in a weepy voice. As Shalu spoke all that, whispering took to new heights and anger was seen on most of the faces.

'Marriage will take place at any cost. It's a matter of my reputation and I have spent four lakh rupees,' Narendra Gupta said loudly, climbing the stage.

'Respectable people don't ask for dowry, Gupta. Marriage will not take place at all,' Shalu's aunty took the reins in her hand and replied from the stage.

'Get out from here. If I call the police, you will be in big trouble,' aunty spoke further.

'I will see you,' Gupta said.

'With pleasure.' You can come anytime to our house and see all of us.' Within next half an hour, the entire drama wrapped up. Only waiters and other workers were busy doing their jobs.

TWENTY FIVE

'What! Oh my God! Nitin spoke on mobile.

'But sometime back, you had told me that everything was going on smoothly,' Nitin extended his sentence.

'Yes, till that time everything was on track,' Shalu said.

'Why did you call me so late?' Nitin asked.

'I was so tensed and distressed that I forgot to call you.' Shalu replied.

'Neither *mummy* nor Reena *di* called me, where have they been?' Nitin shouted.

'Just hold on,' Shalu handed over her mobile to Savitri.

'*Mom*, are you OK?' As Nitin spoke, Savitri broke down loudly and came out of the room. Reena and Vishal followed her.

'Don't cry, *mom*. Everything will be fine.' Nitin said.

'It was Reena, who destroyed everything,' Savitri said, weeping.

'No, *mom*, *di* did the right thing. Just imagine what they could have done after the marriage.' Nitin tried to console his mother.

'This girl has been ominous for us,' as she said, Reena went inside the room weeping. Vishal followed her.

'What are you saying, *mom*? I can't expect this from you. You have always been a source of inspiration for all of us,' Nitin replied. In response, Savitri started weeping again.

'Don't cry, *mummy*. Everything is going to be fine.'

'What else should I do, Nitin? We will have to bear the loss of almost five lakh rupees.' Savitri said.

'Money is not more important than *di*'s life, mom. Whatever stuff we have purchased, it will be used at the time of *di*'s marriage. By the way, how is *papa*?' Nitin spoke.

'He will have to stay in the hospital for a week. Paralysis attack has made his half side immoveable.' Savitri replied.

'What did the doctor say?' Nitin asked.

'Doctor said that it will take a long time for him to recover completely. By the way, what happened in your match?' Savitri changed the topic.

'Last two days were spent in fielding. Most probably I'll be batting tomorrow.' Nitin answered.

'You don't worry and focus on your match,' Savitri spoke.

'OK, give the phone to *di,'* Nitin said.

'Hold on.' Savitri went inside and gave the phone to Reena.

'*Di,* you did the right thing,' Nitin told Reena. In response, Reena started weeping.

'Don't, *di*, don't cry,' Nitin consoled Reena.

'I am responsible for all this,' Reena said.

'No, it was bound to happen. Whatever had to happen, has happened. 'It's OK, *di*. Our team meeting is about to start. I will call you after one hour.' Nitin disconnected the phone as someone had put his hand on Nitin's shoulder.

'Why are you so disappointed and tensed?' a teammate asked.

'No, nothing much. Mom is not well,' Nitin answered, hiding the matter.

TWENTY SIX

Fifteen days later.

'What is the doctor saying?' Nitin was talking to Savitri. He reached back home after finished the tour of one month.

'There is no progress, so far,' she replied.

'But, what does the doctor say?' Nitin asked again in irritation.

'They have told us to give a massage three times a day. *Mom* and uncle have been doing it ever since *papa* came back from the hospital. It has been fifteen days, but there is no sign of improvement,' Reena intervened.

'Oh,' Nitin became more worried.

'Doctors have said that they can't say as how long his paralysed portion will start to respond,' tears started rolling down Reena's cheeks.

'I am more worried about what will happen after next month. The school has given additional fifty thousand rupees along with his salary for two months. Since, it is a private job, your father will not get any more money,' Savitri said.

'We will have to do something. I think we must vacate the first floor to rent it out.' Nitin suggested.

'But, how much earning would come through this. This is a single room.' Savitri replied.

'Even two to three thousand rupees will turn out to be helpful in this condition.' Nitin replied.

'Nitin is right, *mom*. I'll also start giving tuitions.' Reena said.

'I will order a signboard for your coaching class. I am also willing to start something,' Nitin said.

'What and where will the money come from?' Savitri said.

'I have around twenty thousand rupees in my account and soon, I will get my fees for the Ranji matches,' Nitin said.

'What all can be managed in twenty to thirty thousand rupees?' Savitri spoke.

'Let us see mom, what can be done.' Nitin spoke looking at the fan.

TWENTY SEVEN

'Oh! You have come again,' Shalu said with a bit of surprise as she opened the gate.

'Madam, I am just doing my duty,' a courier boy said. He opened his bag and took a small packet and a bouquet to hand over.

'No problem. No need to be worried at all,' Shalu said while signing the receipt.

'Who is this, Shalu?' Shalu's mom, Geeta Gupta, asked.

'No one, mom, my gaga has sent a gift again.' Shalu replied.

'Oh! It's enough now. It's the fifth time in this month that he has sent a gift. Who can this be after all?' Geeta asked.

'I don't know, mom. I am surprised myself,' Shalu said while reading the greeting card closely.

'Are you hiding something from me?' Geeta asked.

'If I had to hide anything from you, then why would I receive these gifts at home in front of you?' Shalu replied.

'Should I ask your father to complain about this to police?' Geeta asked.

'Why are you tensed, mom? If someone gets pleasure in doing this, let him enjoy.' Shalu hugged and kissed on her mother's cheek as she reached the first floor.

'By the way, where are you going? Which perfume have you used? What a fantastic perfume it is,' Shalu's mother said.

Actually Kapil has thrown the party for the more than seventy five per cent marks he got in B.Tech first year. Apart from that, today is his parents' twentieth marriage anniversary as well.

'And he is in U.P. Ranji Trophy team as well, no?' Geeta asked.

'Yes, mom.'

'Hmm! He is a very good combination of sports and studies. He is smart as well.' Geeta spoke.

'Yes, mom.'

'He is suitable for you. Your first year of engineering is cleared with good marks, too.' Geeta smiled.

'Come on, mom, I never saw him from that perspective,' seriousness replaced the smile on Shalu's face.

'Then, you must change your outlook. After all what's the harm in this?' Geeta continued to speak.

'Mom, love just happens and can't be forced. Apart from that, there is a huge difference between our status even our caste is not same', Shalu replied.

But, have you seen how Kapil father treats your father?' Geeta spoke.

'Had he treated *papa* well, he would have invited him for today's party.' Shalu spoke firmly.

'For your kind information, let me tell you that he has given the invitation.' Geeta spoke.

'Oh! That's nice. Let me make a move, mom. I will talk to you about this, later.'

'OK, but think about it seriously.' Geeta said.

'OK, bye, mom.'

'Bye-bye.'

TWENTY EIGHT

'How are you, Shalu?' Kapil was waiting for her for more than half an hour outside his house. His bungalow was glowing with light and a long queue of posh and costly cars were adorning the house.

'I am good, Kapil Tiwari. What about you?' Shalu hugged him.

'Oh! B.M.W.' Shalu became excited as she saw a shining black car within a distance of hardly ten metres.

'Yes, this belongs to Mr. Singhania. His son has also come for the party.' Kapil said.

'It's my dream car,' Shalu said.

'Don't worry, you will have it one day,' Kapil said.

'By the way, come in. I have been waiting for you for long,' Kapil broke her concentration as she was still looking at the car.

'Oh! Sorry, dear. Actually, the B.M.W. took my attention.' She replied. Both started walking towards the house. It was too crowded inside as the guests were pouring in. The waiters and other people were busy in their duty. Music band in the lawn of the bungalow was playing the latest Bollywood songs.

'Shalu, you are looking very hot,' Kapil said.

'Thank you,' Shalu said.

'Mom, Dad, she is Shalu,' Kapil introduced her to his parents as both stepped in.

'*Namaste,* aunty…*Namaste* uncle,' Shalu greeted them one by one folding both her hands.

'Hello, my daughter,' Mr. Dharmendra Tiwari kissed on her forehead and the same was done by his wife.

'Really, you are very beautiful. Kapil keeps talking about you every now and then,' Kapil's mother said.

'Mr. Gupta didn't come?' Kapil's father asked.

'Uncle, he will directly come from office,' Shalu replied.

'OK, by the way, Shalu, what percentage of marks did you get?'

'Eighty six per cent. Uncle'

'Learn something from her, Kapil,' Dharmendra Tiwari said.

'Yes, *papa*. Actually, she is not spending six hours daily in the ground,' Kapil replied.

'Ha-ha-ha! Smart boy. Take her around the house.'

'Ok, *papa*.' Both started to walk on the first floor through stairs. In between, Kapil was greeting the guests and giving instructions to waiters and staff as well.

'Hey, Nitin hasn't reached yet?' Shalu's question changed the expressions on Kapil's face.

"Every time Nitin…I will remove Nitin's name from your mind,' Kapil spoke silently in his mind.

'I had given a call to him almost one hour back. He told me that he would come as soon as the doctor completes his father's routine checkup.' Kapil told Shalu.

'Your room seems to be changed,' Shalu spoke in surprise as both entered.

'No, this is the same room you visited almost ten days back. Since you had given some advice and pointed out somethings, I decided to decorate my room as per your advice,' Kapil spoke with joy.

'Yes, the room is looking far better now.'

'And, the credit goes to you.'

'Thanks a lot.'

'Most welcome,' Kapil greeted her by sitting on his knees.

'Ha-ha-ha-ha…' Shalu burst into laughter.

'What an act…what an act,' Nitin entered the room, clapping, along with Vishal.

'Hey, Nitin, I was waiting for you,' Shalu rushed to Nitin, hugged him and Vishal.

'How is uncle now?' Shalu asked.

'His condition is still the same. I don't know when he will improve?' he said with worry.

'Don't worry. Everything will be OK,' Shalu said.

'Hey, how are you, Jai and Veeru?' Kapil shook hand with both one by one. (He called them Jai, and Veeru. Jai and Veeru are famous characters of a super hit Indian movie, Sholay. Jai and Veeru are known for their friendship).

'Hey, Nitin, what have you worn? You should have been better dressed,' Kapil taunted at him. This comment made the atmosphere a bit serious.

'What's wrong in the dress? He is looking fine,' Shalu came in for Nitin's defense with a huge smile.

'Don't mind, dear. I mean that you are going to be the next Jatin Tendulkar. So, you should maintain your image and standard,' Kapil Tiwari, wearing an expensive black suit, said by sneering at Nitin's clothes. Nitin smiled, but it brought expressions of anger on his face.

'If you have any money problem, then you can purchase from the chor bazaar like you used to do in your childhood days and if…'

'What are you talking about on this day? Come on, let's have a beer,' Shalu hit on Kapil's shoulder before he could complete his sentence.

'Oh yes, why not? Waiter, Waiter,' Kapil called out loudly. Soon, the trio was celebrating in a small room. In between, Kapil three more friends joined the company.

'Hey, Nitin, how's your practice going on?' One of them asked.

'Nice, I have only one target, to play in the next under-nineteen World Cup.' Nitin replied.

'Oh yes, since you failed to break Jatin's record of playing for India before him, then you could have, atleast, got the consolation prize.' Kapil and his friends started laughing. The remaining trio of Nitin, Vishal and Shalu felt uncomfortable with their laughter.

'When will uncle and aunty cut the cake?' Vishal asked looking at his wrist watch with restlessness.

'It will take half an hour,' Kapil said.

'By the way, Nitin, how are your studies going on? I have heard that you failed in B.A. first year,' Kapil passed a comment once again.

'In B.A. first year,' Kapil's friends spoke together with surprise and started laughing loudly.

'Actually,'

'My dear, forget about cricket and just focus on your family. Otherwise, you will be in great trouble. I mean no Jatin Tendulkar and no job.' Kapil spoke.

'Ha-ha-ha-ha...Jatin Tendulkar.... Jatin Tendulkar,' Kapil and his friends laughed so loudly that one of the beer glasses fell on the floor. As the glass was broken, laughter became even louder. But, one sound converted the noise into absolute silence. Shalu stood up and slapped Kapil Tiwari.

'Shalu!' Kapil shouted, keeping a hand on his cheek.

'Have you invited Nitin to insult him, make a mockery of him or to share happiness?' Shalu shouted.

'Sorry...I am very-very sorry, Shalu. I was only pulling his leg in a healthy manner,' Kapil said.

'Is this really a healthy way?' Shalu stared at him.

'Sorry, Nitin. I am sorry friends if you felt bad,' Kapil apologised.

'No problem, mate,' Nitin replied.

'I should make a move now. I have to give a massage to *papa*. This is a small gift from my side for uncle and aunty,' Nitin said, handing over a packet to Kapil Tiwari.

'What is this? You can't go like that without having dinner,' Kapil said and started opening the packet.

'Hey, what is this?' Kapil said with a smile as he saw the gift. His friends were smiling, too, but, with hesitation and looking at Shalu. This time, Shalu was also smiling.

'This is the latest released book about Jatin,' Nitin replied with innocence.

'Now you tell, Shalu, who will not laugh at this? On a marriage anniversary, he has come up with the autobiography of Jatin,' Nitin spoke.

'What's wrong in this?' Nitin asked.

'It's OK, dear. You are absolutely right. Please have dinner and give this gift to mom and *papa* yourself,' Kapil said, folding both the hands. Everyone was smiling at this and the atmosphere became light once again.

'Come on, friends. Let's enjoy.' Everyone came in the lawn, where a band was playing the beats of Bollywood hits and arrangements were made for the cutting of cake and dinner was served.

TWENTY NINE

One week later.

'Kapil was right that day, Nitin,' Shalu spoke to Nitin. Both were talking in the company park.

'What do you mean?' Nitin looked into her eyes.

'You must know at least where are you going?'

'I didn't understand.'

'You came for the party in a track suit. I defended you before them, but I, too, wanted to point out that.'

'You mean, you also felt embarrassed,' Nitin asked.

'You are taking me wrong, Nitin. I wanted you to look like a star amongst.'

'A player becomes a star through his game, not by his clothes.'

'Are you saying that Jatin should not look into the way he dresses? You often appreciate his dress sense as to the sober clothes he wears and his shoes.' Nitin didn't give a reply.

'When you follow Tendulkar passionately, why don't you do it in terms of dress sense?' Shalu said.

'OK, I will keep that in mind.' Nitin replied.

'And, whenever you need money, I will help you in every possible way. By the way, you are not even focusing on your studies,' Shalu stared at him.

'I am doing that, Shalu.'

'Then why you failed in B.A. first year...B.A. first year!'Shalu stressed on the last line after taking a pause for a few seconds.

'You know about the problem I have faced recently,' Nitin said.

'Don't give false logic, Nitin. You took your exams much before your father's mishap,' Nitin kept listening.

'Look at Kapil Tiwari. He just passed B. Tech first year with more than 75 per cent marks. He is doing far better in studies than you. And he is also a part of the Ranji Trophy team,' Shalu said.

'Look at his performance and look at mine,' Nitin spoke.

'Your logic is wrong again. What I mean is that he spends as much time on the ground as you,' Shalu said.

'But my circumstances are different,' Nitin explained.

'Uffffff!It's tough to have a discussion with you. I don't know anything. I just want to see you doing better than Kapil in both the spheres, cricket as well as studies.' Shalu spoke firmly.

'I am trying my best.' Nitin assured.

'It should be reflected in the results as well, Nitin. It's good that you broke Jatin's record of playing Ranji Trophy by playing at a younger age but, what happened after that. Your performance hasn't been up to the mark,' Shalu remarked.

'This year, my performance has improved a lot. I have also been selected in the Duleep Trophy,' Nitin said.

'We all have a lot of expectations from you. In next two years if you don't represent India, it will be tough for you to deal with the circumstances.' Shalu put her neck on his shoulder.

'I know it very well. That's why all my focus is on the next under-nineteen World Cup.'

'Yes, Nitin you will have to play in the World Cup. It's going to be not only yours, but my test as well,' Shalu spoke.

'Everything is going to be fine.' Nitin lay down and put his head in Shalu's lap. He pulled her neck down and started kissing her lips.

THIRTY

Ten days later.

Nitin was giving instructions to the driver of the van.

'Stop here, brother,' Nitin said. 'Come on, Vishal, you, too. Please help us,' Nitin ordered Vishal, who was sitting next to him.

'You have come very early,' Savitri said as she came out of the house hearing Nitin's voice.

'Today is Sunday, mom, so the traffic was not as usual,' Nitin said.

'Take the trolley off the van carefully,' Savitri said.

'There is no need to worry about it, *mom*. I have brought three helpers as well.' Soon, all, except Savitri, were busy in taking a big makeshift shop off the van.

'*Ufffff*! It's too heavy,' Nitin said, wiping out sweat from his face. A huge makeshift shop of steel was set up almost ten metres ahead of Nitin's house.

'Have you made the payment?' Savitri asked.

'Yes, *mom*,' Nitin replied.

'When will the material be supplied?' Savitri asked.

'Aunty, I spoke to Rashid *bhai* (brother) just a few minutes back. He assured me that the material will be sent by 8:00 p.m.' Vishal said.

'OK, that's good. It means that the business can be started from tomorrow,' Savitri said.

'Yes, why not? We shouldn't waste time at all,' Vishal said.

'Hey, what are you doing Savitri *ji*?' One neighbour asked as many had gathered seeing the makeshift shop getting unloaded.

'It would be known to all, tomorrow, Sharma *Ji,'* Savitri went inside her house.'

* * *

The next day, in evening, Nitin and Vishal were busy decorating the makeshift shop.

'Vishal, take these posters and stick on the either side of the shop,' Nitin said.

'Jatin's poster,' Vishal said with a surprise from the roof of the shop.

'Yes, I have made these special posters. It would attract customers,' Nitin replied.

'Oh God! Jatin is involved even in this matter,' Vishal remarked.

'You know, *yaar* (friend), he is my God and I start any work by taking his name,' Nitin spoke.

'It's OK.' Vishal started sticking posters on the upper part of the shop.

'It's really looking very nice. I am pretty much sure that none of the shops will be like ours in this colony,' Nitin said beholding the shop.

'Will you keep gazing at the shop only, or put the things in?' Savitri said.

'Oh! Yes, come on, Vishal. We must start doing the main job.' Within minutes, both started taking out the big boxes from Nitin's house.

'Carefully, Nitin or else the money will be wasted,' Savitri, who was monitoring, said. Almost thirty boxes were put inside the shop and both, Nitin and Vishal, opened the bags. They took trays out of the box and kept them in the front row.

'Hey Nitin, will you sell eggs now?' One voice interrupted them.

'Why? Do you have any problem Sharma *ji*?' Savitri intervened.

'No, I don't have any problem. But, what will people say, that future Jatin is selling eggs!'

'When we are not worried about this, who are you to comment? Just mind your own business,' Savitri reprimanded him.

Neighbour Sharma ji went away, but many people gathered around the shop and started whispering. Soon, the news spread in the locality that Nitin has opened an egg shop. 'Hey, did you hear that Nitin opened a shop of eggs?' 'Hey, Nitin opened a shop of eggs!!' 'The next Jatin opened a shop of eggs!!'

* * *

'What! He has opened a shop of eggs. Are you sure?' Kapil said, when one of his friends, Dinesh, told him about Nitin's shop.

'Yes, Kapil, I have seen it myself.'

'That's good. Now this eggey has done my job easier,' Kapil spoke.

'Who, the eggey?' Dinesh asked.

'Nitin, the eggey, Dinesh, Nitin, the eggey!' Kapil looked into his eyes.

'Ha-ha-ha-ha, you have given a good name to Nitin. Nitin, the eggey!' Both were laughing loudly.

'By the way, which job were you talking about?' Dinesh asked.

'Now, it will be easy for me to get Shalu,' Kapil said.

'How?' Dinesh asked.

'You are a donkey. Just wait and you will see that she will be mine,' Kapil spoke in happiness.

'Best of luck, Dear! I am always with you,' Dinesh showed thumbs up to Kapil Tiwari.

THIRTY ONE

Five days later.

Kapil gave a call to Shalu.

'Hello Shalu, how are you?' Kapil spoke.

Hi Kapil, I am fine. How are you? So, how is life going on.' Shalu asked.

'Nothing, now the focus is on studies, as the Ranji Trophy session is over,' Kapil replied.

'OK.'

'How is Nitin doing?' Kapil asked.

'Actually, I haven't met him for a long time because I have come to Lucknow to spend some quality time with my cousins,' Shalu replied.

'Are you talking from Lucknow?' Kapil asked.

'Yes,'

'When are you coming back to Kanpur?'

'Day after tomorrow, as I have to take admission in the fashion designing course,' Shalu said.

'What will you do after all, engineering, dancing, swimming, fashion designing,' Kapil remarked.

'I have so many dreams to fulfill. Still many things are left to do,' Shalu said.

'By the way, I had called you to say sorry, 'Kapil said.

'For what?' Shalu asked.

'For what happened in the party the other day,' Kapil replied.

'Oh! Actually, I was about to say sorry to you Kapil,' Shalu said.

'Sorry, for what?' Kapil asked.

'For that, what you received from my hand?' Shalu said.

'Ha-ha-ha-ha, but I didn't even wash my face ever since I got your slap,' Kapil said.

'Ha-ha-ha-ha-ha' This time Shalu was grinning.

'Though, it was another special reason as well to call you up,' Kapil said.

'What?'

'It's a top secret. When you come back, then I'll tell you?' Kapil replied.

'It seems to be very special,' Shalu spoke.

'Yes, because it's related to your dream,' Kapil said.

'Really?' A crack was felt in her voice.

'Yes, and I will wait for you to come back day after tomorrow.'

'Sure, I will come between 7 and 8 p.m. Bye-bye and take care,' Shalu said.

'Bye-bye,' Kapil said.

THIRTY TWO

Two days later.

'You, too, must have done something in summer vacations,' Shalu was talking to Kapil in his room.

'It's tough for me to take out time for studies. In summers, we have to spend more time in the field. When did you come from Lucknow?' Kapil asked.

'Around 5 o'clock in the evening,' Shalu replied.

'OK. Did you meet Nitin or any other friend?' Kapil stared at her to notice her expressions.

'Not, so far. I slept for two hours and as I got your call, I headed straight to your house,' Shalu replied.

'Hmm,' Kapil whispered.

'By the way, you were talking about something related to my dreams,' Shalu said.

'Oh yes, please come with me.' Both got up and came out of the room.

'Where are we going?' Shalu asked with curiosity.

'Be patient. It's a matter of only five minutes.' Within minutes, they reached at the back side of the bungalow, where at least two dozen cars were parked.

'Oh! What beautiful cars,' Shalu said as she passed in front of them.

'Come on, these are old ones. I have got a special car,' Kapil said.

'Which one?' Shalu asked in excitement.

'It is parked in the last.' As Kapil said that, Shalu caught up speed.

'Wow! Amazing! Brand new BMW!' Shalu was overwhelmed. It's my favourite colour. When did you purchase it?' Shalu's face was shining.

'*Papa* had booked this on my special request. By the way, come, sit inside and take the feel of it,' Kapil said by opening the door. Shalu sat in the front seat.

'Wow!! Kapil, thank you very much. I never thought that I will ever sit in a BMW. It was my dream, Kapil! It was my dream!' Shalu's eyes were shining. Passion could easily be felt by looking at her face.

'And, today, your dream has come true,' Kapil spoke.

'Yes, and I hope one day, I will purchase it,' Shalu said.

'I wish you purchase it as early as possible. By the way, consider this BMW as yours only.'

'Thank you very much, Kapil, for giving me such an honour,' Shalu hugged him.

'I want to take you on a long drive,' Kapil said.

Long drive! At this time! Papa will come early from office. He will scold me,' Shalu replied.

'It's OK. Then, let's go for a short drive,' Kapil spoke.

Kapil started the car and drived it out of bungalow.

'Where would you like to go?' Kapil asked Shalu.

'We should move towards Green Park. These, roads are very wide and the area is peaceful, too,' Shalu said.

'OK. By the way, would you like to meet Nitin?' Kapil played his game!

'Yes. That's a very good idea,' Kapil turned his BMW to the left side instead of right. A mischievous smile was flashing on his face as his plan was getting executed at his will.

'Hey, what is this shop in front of Nitin's house?' Shalu asked, seeing it from a distance of almost from fifty metres.

'I don't know about this,' Kapil shrugged his shoulder.

'Hey, this is a shop for selling eggs.' Kapil stopped his car close to the makeshift shop, deliberately.

'Shalu, I am willing to eat some eggs. Would you like to eat, too?' Kapil asked Shalu while closing the gate.

'Hmmm, I will share with you,' Shalu replied.

'Is anyone in the shop?' Kapil called out loudly.

'Hey, Nitin, this is you! This is your shop,' Kapil acted as if he didn't know anything.

'Hey, Shalu, look, Nitin has opened up a shop.' As Kapil said that, Shalu's face lost shine.

'Hey, come quickly and congratulate Nitin,' Kapil was trying his best to rub salt on their wounds.

'How are you, Nitin?' Shalu asked with a sad face and low esteem in her tone.

'I am fine. Why are you so sad?' Nitin looked into her eyes.

'Not, at all. Actually, you didn't tell me about your new business,' Shalu spoke.

'Oh! You were out of city. Moreover, it was decided and executed within four days,' Nitin replied.

'Who decided about it?' Shalu stared at him.

'Vishal and me proposed this to mother and she gave a green signal.' Nitin was still ignorant about Shalu's sadness, but Kapil knew it all and, was very happy within.

'By the way, please eat the eggs. You have come here for the first time.' Nitin offered two plates. Six eggs were there in each plate.

'I will not eat as am not feeling well,' Shalu pushed the plate back.

'But, I will definitely eat,' Kapil started to eat immediately. This scenario was giving too much pleasure to him.

'What happened?, Nitin asked with innocence.

'I am not feeling well from inside,' Shalu said.

'Would you take anything sweet or a cold drink?' Nitin asked.

'No, I want to go back as soon as possible,' Shalu said. 'Will you not meet *mummy* and Reena *di*? Nitin asked.

'I will come tomorrow, but not at this time,' Shalu replied.

'OK, Nitin give us permission to go, and congratulations, once again, for your new business,' Kapil extended his hand after gulping the sixth egg.

'By the way, your eggs were very tasty. But, I am more impressed with the posters,' Kapil said.

'Thanks, Kapil Tiwari,' Nitin said.

'OK, bye, Nitin,' Shalu said half heartedly.

'Bye-bye.'

'Why are you looking so dejected, Shalu? What happened to you within minutes?' Kapil asked through his sun glasses while driving the car.

'Nothing, Kapil Tiwari, I am not feeling well,' Shalu replied.

'OK, then the drive stands cancelled,' Kapil spoke.

'Sure, we will go some other day,' Shalu said.

'As you wish,' Kapil shrugged. He dropped Shalu outside the gate of her house. He was very happy because he had hit the bull's eye.

THIRTY THREE

Next day.

'You did not find any other work to do,' Shalu spoke to Nitin in the famous park of Kanpur.

'What's wrong in this Shalu?' Nitin asked.

'Do you know that you have become a subject of mockery in the locality? People are laughing at you?' Shalu stared at him with annoyance.

'People don't run my house. Will these people bear my expenses? I don't care for fucking people,' Nitin also spoke in anger.

'But, I do. It's painful for me when they whisper and laugh at you. You could have done some other work, no?' Shalu spoke.

'What other work?' Nitin said.

'There are so many part time jobs available,' Shalu suggested.

'I don't have time during the day. I will have to spend more time in the ground in the coming days' Nitin replied.

'You didn't even consult me on this. If you required money, you could have asked me,' Shalu spoke.

'It's not my matter, Shalu. It's a time of crisis for my entire family. My father is not getting his salary,' Nitin spoke.

'You are right. But, had you told me earlier, we would have planned something better,' Shalu said.

'Vishal and I will expand this business together. If it clicked, we will purchase land to run a poultry farm,' Nitin told Shalu.

'*Uffff*! Why don't you understand, Nitin?' Shalu spoke in anger.

'What is it that I don't understand?' Nitin asked.

'You don't understand that social status is also important. This work has brought a kind of disrespect for you, and for me, as well.' Shalu expressed concern.

'Why for you?' Nitin asked.

What the hell? People have started calling me "eggey's girl friend" in my absence. Soon, they will start saying it directly,' Shalu spoke.

'You should be proud of me that I am earning with honesty,' Nitin said.

'Go to hell with this honesty. There are so many other ways to work with honesty,' Shalu replied.

'What do you want?' Nitin asked.

'I want that you to close the egg shop and do something else,' Shalu spoke.

'That will be difficult for me, Shalu. Even my mom does not feel any kind of embarrassment. Nitin spoke with confidence.

'It means that there is no importance of what I feel,' Shalu spoke.

'Why are you making a small issue so complicated?' Nitin said.

'It's not a small issue for me, Nitin. What will I tell my parents if I have to talk to them regarding us, in future? Should I say that my boy friend runs an egg shop?' Shalu spoke.

'You don't have to get humiliated because of me, Shalu. You should focus on your parents,' Nitin said.

'Go to hell!' Shalu got up and started walking.

'Shalu…hey, Shalu,' Nitin ran behind her. But, she paced up her steps and left the park.

THIRTY FOUR

Ten days later.

5:00 p.m.

'Today, you are looking very smart, Shalu,' Kapil spoke to Shalu at his bungalow, after taking a sip of his Black Label whisky.

'Thanks, Kapil,' Shalu replied.

'Finally, you came for the long drive,' spoke Kapil.

'Actually, I wanted to go that day. But....leave it,' Shalu stopped while speaking something. This brought a smile on Kapil's face.

'Yes, I can understand,' Kapil said while pouring water in her drink.

'By the way, how long will you take?' Shalu gazed at his wrist watch.

'Let's have one peg more,' Kapil replied.

'No, I have drunk enough,' Shalu spoke.

'Come on, one peg more,' Kapil forced.

'OK, but not after this,' Shalu agreed.

'OK, darling, OK.' Having said that Kapil got up and switched on the music player. Songs from the Hindi movie, Devdas-Hamesha he tumko chaha-started to play.

'Hmm, you are feeling romantic,' Shalu smiled looking at him.

'Yes, why not? We are alone here. It's indeed a very romantic atmosphere,' Kapil said while looking through the window.

'Hmmm, you are becoming naughty. By the way, how is your girlfriend doing?' Shalu asked.

'She is fine,' Kapil replied.

'OK, tell me, how does she look and what does she do?' Shalu asked in curiosity.

'She is very beautiful, and studying engineering,' Kapil replied.

'Oh! That's great. Where does she live?' Shalu took a sip from her drink.

'She lives in the next colony,' Kapil said.

'What is her name?' Within seconds, seriousness sported her face and smile converted into curiosity with a little bit of fear on her face. She was staring at him with the glass in her hand.

'Hmmm, you want to know everything in one day. Have patience, dear,' Kapil dodged.

'No, I want to know your girlfriend's name.' Shalu put her glass on the table and stood up.

'I will tell you after some days,' Kapil replied.

'No, I want to know her name now only,' Shalu insisted.

'OK. I will tell you my girlfriend's name but, there is one condition to it,' Kapil spoke.

'What condition?' Shalu asked.

'You will have to dance with me,' Kapil replied moving his eyes in a naughty manner.

'But, we are getting late for the drive, Kapil,' Shalu said.

'We can't go on a long drive,' Kapil spoke.

'But, why can't we?' Shalu looked surprised.

'Just look through the window,' Kapil spoke.

'Oh my God! It's raining heavily,' Shalu spoke after looking out from the window.

'You should not have any problem now,' spoke Kapil Tiwari.

'OK my dear, play the song,' Shalu said.

'Yeah, that's good!' Kapil threw his fists in the air and spoke in aloud voice as if he took a wicket. Soon, both were dancing in the room. Kapil was in a T-shirt and shorts while Shalu had worn a red mini skirt. Kapil tightened his right hand on her back and both were moving on the tune of the song. By then, Black Label whisky had started to throw its impact in Shalu's eyes.

'You seem to be intoxicated,' Kapil started executing his plan.

'Really!' Shalu spoke.

'Yes,' Kapil turned her around and, this time, Shalu's back was touching his front.

'Though, you are becoming smarter day by day,' Shalu remarked.

'It's because of you,' Kapil said.

'Naughty boy!' Both danced for almost ten minutes. During the dance, Kapil's breath, fragrance of his expensive perfume and the effect of Black Label whisky, loosened Shalu's nervous system. After a few minutes, she dropped herself in his arm. Kapil started kissing on her lips passionately. Kapil kept sucking her lips for next few minutes until the song was over.

'Kapil!' Shalu gave a tight slap on his face and pushed him back as her senses made her realise that she was being kissed by Kapil Tiwari.

'What did you do, Kapil?' Shalu was furious.

'Sorry, Shalu, I am very sorry. But, you are my girl friend,' Kapil spoke.

'What! No, Kapil,' Shalu spoke firmly.

'Yes, Shalu, yes. You wanted to know my girl friend's name. Listen, my girl friend's name is Shalu Gupta,' Kapil spoke with conviction in his voice.

'What are you saying, Kapil Tiwari?'

'Yes, Shalu. You have been my dream girl from class ninth,' Kapil spoke.

'But, Kapil, you know that Nitin......'

'Let me tell you that all the greeting cards and other stuff you got, were sent by none other than me,' tears started rolling down Kapil's cheeks. Shalu was looking at his face with surprise.

'Yes, Shalu, I love you since our childhood. I have always dreamt of spending my life with you. Once you mentioned about BMW, I forced my father to purchase the same. It was only for you, Shalu, only for you.' Tears rolled down from Shalu's eyes, too.

'But, you know that I am in love with Nitin,' Shalu spoke.

'No, Shalu, you are telling lies. Had you been in love with Nitin, this wouldn't have happened,' replied Nitin.

'It happened because of wine,' Shalu said.

'No, Shalu, it happened because your love for Nitin is fading away. I will give you everything that Nitin will never be able to.' Shalu was absolutely stunned.

'I want to go back home, Kapit,' Shalu requested.

'But,'

'Yes, it has stopped raining,' Shalu looked through the window and spoke.

'Please stay for more time,' Nitin asked.

'No, I have to rush back immediately,' Shalu replied.

'OK, I will drop you to your house,' Kapil said.

'No, Kapil, not today, at least,' Shalu said.

'OK, as you wish.' Shalu left Kapil's room. He accompanied her till the gate of his bungalow.

THIRTY FIVE

Next morning, Shalu was combing her hair in front of a huge mirror in her room. Suddenly, she stopped and, was lost in some thoughts, looking at the mirror.

Shalu (looking at her image in the mirror): 'Kapil loves me deep from his heart!'

Mirror image: 'But, you love Nitin, Shalu. He loves you, too.'

Shalu: But, I never ever saw much passion in his eyes as Kapil Tiwari.

Mirror: 'May be he doesn't believe in showing off. They may be different in nature.'

Shalu: 'Kapil will give me all that I have always dreamt about, a huge bungalow, expensive cars, ravishing life style and everything else.'

Mirror: 'Nitin is future super star of Indian cricket. He can also give you everything.'

Shalu: 'What has he given me so far? He has never given me a good gift in so many years, although I gave him far expensive gifts.'

Mirror: 'Why are you comparing Nitin with Kapil Tiwari? Have you ever done this in all these years?'

Shalu: 'That was the matter of my childhood.'

Mirror: 'That means, Nitin is your true and first love.'

Shalu: 'But, I will have to see my future as well.'

Mirror: 'Nitin, too, can give you a good future?'

Shalu: 'Will he give me a good future through his egg shop? He has even failed in his B.A. first year. What will he do, even if he completes graduation?'

Mirror: 'You are being selfish.'

Shalu: 'I am being practical.'

'Hey, Shalu what are you looking at in mirror,' suddenly her mother intervened.

'Nothing, *mummy*, nothing.'

'No, something has definitely happened. I have been observing you for long. Are you OK?' her mother touched her forehead and checked her pulse.

'I am fine, mom.'

'Hmmm, have you fallen in love with someone?' Shalu's mother asked.

'Come on, mom,'

'If that happens, do inform me. We will not hesitate in moving ahead with the proposal if the boy is as good as Kapil Tiwari,' Shalu's mother spoke.

'No, *mummy*. It is not like that, at all. Actually, I hit the bed late in the night. It's because of that,' Shalu said.

'OK, then take proper rest and don't go to college.'

'OK, *mummy*, I am also not willing to go.' Shalu replied.

THIRTY SIX

After Few days.

'Are you still angry with me?' Nitin asked having kissed on Shalu's forehead. She was lying in Nitin's lap in the famous Kanpur Park.

Yes, I was angry, but not right now. she replied.

'But, you seem to be angry,' Nitin asked.

'How can you say so?' Shalu asked.

'Because, I am missing that love and passion in your eyes, what I have seen before,' Nitin replied.

'It's not like that, darling,' Shalu sat up and kissed on Nitin lips.

'I know that you are feeling insulted because of me. But, let me assure you that one day you will be proud of me,' Nitin spoke.

'I know my sweet heart,' she kissed on his lips again.

'By the way, what are you doing on 24th April?' Nitin asked.

'After three days. Hmmm…nothing, but I have to go somewhere,' Shalu said.' I think you have forgotten me,' Nitin replied.

'Come on, you have started again,' Shalu spoke.

'Yes, because I am being compelled to remind you about 24th April for the first time,' Nitin said.

'Hmmm, Oh sorry, I am sorry. I forgot that it is your birthday on 24th April,' Shalu said recalling.

'Yes, and this is the first time in last five years that you have forgotten it,' Nitin said.

'I said sorry, Nitin. Actually, these days, I am tensed,' Shalu spoke.

'That's why I said that you have forgotten me,' Nitin spoke.

'If you talk like that, I will walk away,' she said in anger.

'OK, dear, Ok…Sit in my lap,' Nitin dragged her close to himself and started kissing on her cheek and lips.

'By the way, what is the plan?' Shalu asked.

'You tell. For last five years everything has been taking place according to you,' Nitin said.

'Hmmm, then the celebration will take place at the park again,' Shalu replied.

'Then, start giving invitations to all the friends,' Nitin said.

'You send invitations. I will take care of the arrangement of the restaurant,' Shalu said.

'OK, but this time, no restaurant,' Nitin said.

'Why?' Shalu asked with surprise.

'Because, this time I have decided to celebrate in a special way,' Nitin spoke.

'What special?' Shalu asked.

'You know that Jatin and my birthday fall on the same date. Jatin is going to be thirty, while I will turn eighteen,' Nitin spoke.

'Then, what? What is new this time?' Shalu asked.

'Our group, Vishal, me and some other friends from the colony have decided to celebrate in a grand style. We will celebrate in the park this time,' Nitin spoke.

'But, it will turn out to be costly,' Shalu expressed.

'We have collaborated with the Jatin fan club and they have agreed,' Nitin spoke.

'That's good. It will be great fun,' Shalu spoke in excitement.

'Yes, I want to celebrate this birthday as if it were my last one,' Nitin said.

'What are you saying?' She looked at him with surprise.

'Don't worry. I am not going anywhere. You know my biggest challenge will start from this session,' Nitin spoke.

'Yes, I know that you have only one session left to fulfill your dreams,' Shalu remarked.

'Yes, Shalu, the upcoming under-nineteen World Cup is my life. I will work hard day and night, and leave no stone unturned to fulfill my dream,' Nitin said, contemplating.

'OK, I think I should move as I have to start the preparations,' Nitin spoke further.

'OK, I also have to go for my dance class,' Shalu spoke.

'Just one minute,' Nitin held her hand, turned her face and started kissing on her lips.

THIRTY SEVEN

Three days later

Arrangements were at their peak. A group of twenty to twenty five youngsters were busy giving shape to the celebrations marking Nitin and Jatin's birthday.

'Hey, Vishal, stick that poster properly,' Shalu pointed out towards Jatin's poster. 'Oh, I just stuck it,' Vishal turned back and stuck the poster properly.

'When will the cake be cut?'

'We are ready. Let the media men and photographers come.'

'Kapil hasn't come so far.' Vishal gazed at his wrist watch.

'He is about to reach with Dinesh and Shyam,' Shalu replied.

'OK,' Vishal became busy with work again. After almost twenty minutes, Kapil entered with three of his friends.

'Hey, Kapil Tiwari, how are you?' Shalu rushed to him and welcome him by hugging. Soon, he was surrounded by all his friends.

'I am fine, darling,' Kapil spoke.

'You are looking dashing,' Shalu complimented.

'And you, gorgeous. By the way, where is eggey?' Kapil passed a remark on Nitin.

'Eggey, who eggey?' Shalu said with surprise.

'Nitin, the eggey,' as he said, a burst of laughter took place.

'Hey, come on, you will not change, no?' Shalu said.

'Friends, today is eighteenth birthday of my best friend and future super star, Nitin Srivastava, and the greatest, Jatin Tendulkar. So, please give a big hand to Nitin and Jatin,' as Shalu announced, the noise of clapping echoed in the fold.

'I would like to invite Nitin to cut the cake,' Shalu said. Nitin came to the centre.

'Dear friends, thank you very much that you came for me,' having said that, Nitin started cutting the cake. Shalu tried to put the cake into his mouth but, he stopped her.

'What happened?' Shalu asked.

'To God, first,' Nitin replied.

'Oh sorry, I forgot,' Shalu said by smiling.

Nitin turned to Jatin's photo, which was placed on the table. He touched the piece of cake on Jatin's lips.

'Happy birthday to you, Jatin.... Happy birthday to you, Nitin,' the sound of clapping started echoing once again.

'Hey, friends, thank you very much for coming. I will not take much time as I know what you all are waiting for. Please enjoy,' as Shalu said, everyone dispersed and formed groups of four and five friends together. Some were dancing while others were chatting.

'Hey, Nitin, have you made my arrangement?' Kapil said winking.

'Hey, Kapil Tiwari, why are you asking this from eggey? He hardly earns two hundred rupees daily.' As Dinesh spoke, Vishal and Nitin stared at him. Shalu was stunned, too, but Kapil was smiling.

'Yes, I have made arrangements. I have brought one tin beer,' Nitin replied.

'Come on, eggey, you don't have to worry about us. We have brought our quota.'

'Hey, eggey, take this and bring it out from the car.' Dinesh threw the car's key to Nitin.

'Hey, what is this way of talking to him?' Vishal intervened before Nitin reacted.

'Why are you coming between us?'

'I am just saying that you shouldn't talk to him in this manner. Everyone is watching. Don't forget, you have come to congratulate him,' Vishal spoke.

'It's between both of us. When Nitin doesn't have any problem, why do you?' Kapil spoke.

'I am only saying that you should not talk to Nitin like that,' Vishal said in a loud voice and charged. Everyone stopped their activities and became attentive.

'Stop Vishal,' Shalu tried to push him. Nitin also rushed to hold Vishal.

'What will you do?'

'If you say anything, you will face the consequences,' Vishal shouted. Shalu and Nitin were trying their best to push him.

'Hey, bastard, eggey, you haven't brought the Black Label from the car till now.' Dinesh spoke.

'Bastard,' Vishal pushed Shalu aside and rushed to catch Dinesh. Vishal put a cracking slap on Dinesh's face. Within seconds, fighting scene from some Bollywood movie was created. Both were giving punches to each other. By then, the remaining friends also gathered around them and were trying their best to separate them, except one, Kapil Tiwari, who was just enjoying the act. A strange smile was flashing on his face as if his plan was executing the way he had wanted.

'Enough is enough. You have spoiled the party,' Kapil gave a tight slap on Dinesh's face. Kapil's reaction reduced his frowns.'

'Sorry, Vishal and Nitin. I am sorry on behalf of him,' Kapil acted.

'Come on, forget it and hug Nitin,' Kapil instructed him. Both hugged each other, but it was nothing less than a drama.

'Come on, guys. Nothing happened. Enjoy the party,' the atmosphere became light as Shalu announced this. In between, Nitin brought the Black Label whisky and everyone started to enjoy the party again.

THIRTY EIGHT

The following day.

Kapil and Dinesh were talking at former's bungalow.

'I will not spare him, Kapil Tiwari,' Dinesh said after taking one sip of whisky. 'Calm down, dear, calm down. That slap was on my face as well, not only yours. After all you went with me despite not being invited,' Kapil said.

'Then, what have you thought about it?' Dinesh asked.

'You must keep patience, Dinesh. We should wait for the right time.' Kapil replied.

'You don't know, Kapil Tiwari. I couldn't sleep the whole night. Firstly, they insulted me by not inviting me to the function, and then…' Dinesh's face became tight and he hit his fist on his left palm with anger, fuck off,' he spoke.

'Cool down, brother,' Kapil caught his hand and rubbed his palm.

'This son of a peon is nothing before us,' Dinesh said grinning.

'Dear, that was their place. Had it been in our party, Vishal wouldn't have gone back to his house alive.'

'By the way, what is the time?' Kapil looked at his wrist watch.

'It is fifteen minutes past three.'

'You should move out now. Shalu can come anytime.' Kapil told Dinesh.

'What! Shalu is coming?' Dinesh exclaimed.

'Yes. Actually, I had to discuss the second year course with her,' Kapil replied.

'Oh!'

'By the way, you don't worry about it any more. I have a plan for you.' Kapil spoke.

'What plan?' Dinesh asked.

'I will tell you later in detail. It will benefit you.' Kapil assured.

'OK,' Dinesh said in a thinking mode.

'OK, bye, I will call you.' Kapil hugged Dinesh and he left the bungalow.

* * *

'Why did you come so late?' Kapil said with a bit of anger.

'Actually, some guests had come over. So I was busy attending them,' Shalu said.

'Are you ready now?' Kapil asked.

'Yes, by the way, where is aunty?' Shalu asked.

'She has gone to attend a kitty party. I am coming in five minutes and you stay here till then. OK,' Kapil said.

'OK,' Shalu replied.

Kapil left the room and, within five minutes, he returned in the BMW.

'OK, darling, come,' as Kapil called out, Shalu came out of the room.

'Wow! It looks like as if it was purchased yesterday only, whereas it has been more than two months now.' Shalu's eyes were lit up as she saw the BMW.

'I wash it two times a day, personally, ever since it was purchased.' Kapil said.

'Why? You have so many servants.' Shalu spoke.

'Because, it's very close to my heart.' Kapil said.

'Why?'

'Because, it's your dream car.'

'We should move now, no?'

'OK, madam.' Soon, Kapil and Shalu were on their way a long drive. It was around 6:00 p.m.

'Thanks a lot, Shalu. Finally, you fulfilled your promise,' Kapil said while driving.

'It's nothing compared to what you did.' Shalu spoke.

'What did I do?' Kapil said, feeling surprised.

'First, you realised my dream, secondly, you fulfilled it within a week.' Shalu spoke with gratitude.

'Not a big deal for me. After all what will my father do with so much money? Being the only son, I also have few rights in the house.' Kapil said.

'Why few, you have all the rights. After all for whom is uncle earning. Who else is there to use this expensive car and a huge bungalow after him?' Shalu said.

'That's why I said that it is not a big deal for me. I did it only for you.'

'But, for me it's a very big deal, Kapil.'

'OK, by the way, how are you feeling?'

'Very nice, I am living my dream.'

'Tell me, what is your dream apart from this?' Kapil looked into her eyes.

'What do you mean?'

'I mean, what more do you want to achieve in your life?' Kapil said.

I want to achieve all that anyone wants, like, bungalow, car, a good bank balance and to become wife of a superstar.'

'OK,'

'Don't you think you expect too much,' Kapil spoke again after a pause.

'Everyone does. I am not an exceptional case,' Shalu replied.

'Hmmm, yes, you are right. There is no limit to dreaming,' Kapil said.

'Yes, no limit.' Shalu smiled at him.

'Hey, why did you stop the car?' Shalu spoke with surprise as Kapil stopped the car. It was dark in that area. Hardly any car was visible on that road. Even if any car passed through, it came in a gap of almost ten minutes.

'Yes, I stopped as it was necessary.' Kapil caught her hand. There was a strange licentiousness in his eyes, which brought fear on Shalu's face.

'What are you doing Kapil Tiwari?' Shalu said in a shivering voice.

'I want to make love to you, Shalu.' Kapil locked the door through the automatic system as she tried to open the gate. Kapil dragged Shalu close to him.

'I will cry out, Kapil.'

'Cry at your best. No one will come here,' Kapil spoke with some animosity.

'Please, Kapil, for God's sake,' Kapil started laughing loudly as Shalu tried to touch his feet. Shalu was stunned.

'Hey, why are you laughing like mad?' Shalu spoke in disgust.

'You got scared, no?' Kapil repeated this line many times while laughing.

'Bastard, dog…it means that you were acting,' Shalu punched on his back and head many times. Her fear was converted into a sweet anger. Kapil was trying to save himself by covering his head with both the hands.

'Were you really scared?' Kapil said, when the situation became normal.

'Yes,'

'How can you think I can do like that?'

'I don't know. Perhaps this was a situation you created just to scare me. Look at this area, no one can be seen here, any girl would be scared,' Shalu said.

'Hmmmm,'

'Actually I was just kidding. By the way, I stopped the car for some other reason.'

What reason?' Surprise arrested her face again.

'I wanted to give you something,'

'What'

'Close your eyes, first,'

'Hmmm, OK,'

'And don't open, until I ask you to,' Kapil said.

'OK, dear, OK.'

'Open your eyes now,' After two minutes, Kapil permitted her to open her eyes.

'Wow! It's beautiful,' Shalu said as she saw a ring in her middle finger.

'This is really amazing,' Shalu was still observing it.

'Yes, and this is only for you. My purpose to take you with me on a long drive was this,' Kapil smiled.

'Thank you so much, Kapil. You have been so nice,'

'No need to say thanks. It is an honour for me.'

'By the way, I want to give you one more thing,'

'What? This is enough, Kapil,'

'Only one more thing,'

'What is that?'

'Just close your eyes once again and don't open until, I say, OK.'

'OK, dear, OK.'

'Promise,'

'Promise,' Shalu said.

As Shalu closed her eyes, Kapil came close to her and started kissing on her lips. He grabbed her head from behind and kept sucking her lips. He put her clothes off. Shalu was looking sexy in black bra. Kapil unhooked her bra as well. By pushing the button, he unfolded the seat completely and it was converted into a bed. Within minutes, Shalu was lying on the seat. Kapil started sucking her b***s passionately. Shalu, too, was responding to him.

It was little bit strange that the girl who was afraid of being raped just a couple of minutes back, surrendered herself before the same person. For next twenty minutes or so, Kapil kept sucking Shalu's lips, b***s, and licked her thighs as well. The car was buzzing with hot breath. After, almost twenty minutes, Kapil tried to put his hand in Shalu's panty. But as his hand touched the panty, Shalu caught his hand. Kapil Tiwari, too, didn't force and kept sucking and playing with the upper portion of Shalu's body. During this period, Shalu fulfilled her promise, she didn't open her eyes.

THIRTY NINE

Ten days later.

'Hey, what is the price of six boiled eggs? a smart, handsome man, around twenty five years of age, asked Nitin and Vishal. It was around 9 p.m.

'Eighteen rupees,' Nitin replied.

'Did you hear guys?' the young man shouted loudly.

'No,' the word buzzed with so many voices, simultaneously, from a car that stopped almost in front of the shop.

'Come on friend. You can find the egg, two rupees per piece anywhere.'

'Brother, there is a huge difference in our stuff and other shops,' Vishal said. +

'Really!'

'Yes, a lot of difference,' Nitin supported.

'It's OK. Please prepare six plates with ten eggs in each,' the young man ordered.

'OK, it will take ten minutes,'

'No problem, I am sitting in the car. Do you have any problem if we drink a bit?' young man gesticulated.

'Not outside, brother. People of the colony will object. You can drink inside your car by parking in a corner,' Vishal replied.

'Thank you.' After few minutes, a small party was going on in the car, while Nitin and Vishal became busy in the shop. The party continued till almost 10:30 p.m. Around that time, Vishal went to them.

'Hey, brother, have you eaten?' No one turned upto him, out of the two persons who sat in the front seat. Light music was on and all were laughing loudly.

'Brother, have you eaten?' Vishal asked again.

'Oh, yes,' the young man turned upto Vishal after hearing his voice.

'Please return all the plates and you should move now,' Vishal ordered.

'Why move? Do you have any problem?'

'Actually, the police jeep can come any time. It's the patrolling time for them,'

'Fuck off the police. They can't do anything to us, my child,' one boy, sitting on the back seat, replied.

'I am warning all of you all. Rest is your wish,' Vishal said shrugging his shoulders.

'Take these, your plates.' the young man returned the plates.

Sir, one hundred and eight rupees,'

'What will you do with one hundred and eight rupees? A boy, from the back seat, said loudly under the effect of alcohol.

'He will fuck his mother with this money,' another boy replied immediately even before Vishal opened his mouth.

'How are you talking, sir?' Vishal replied.

'I will talk in the same way. What will you do? Will you fuck your mother with this amount? Go away from here. We will not give you the money.'

'Mind your language, otherwise..., Vishal stopped.

'What otherwise....What otherwise,' this time the young man, who sat on the front seat, spoke with anger.

'Make your friend understand, sir,' Vishal replied.

'Go away from here,' the young man gave a slap on Vishal's face.

'Bastard, stop here for a while, and I will fuck you,'

'Bastard, you are challenging me,' the young man pushed Vishal, opened the gate and got down.

'Everyone, come out. He deserves to be taught a lesson,' as the young man said that, all six boys came out of the car. Three of them were holding hockey sticks and two had iron rods. It was dark on the road and most of the people were inside their house.

'What were you saying, dog?' One boy said that giving a slap on Vishal's face by grabbing his collar. Soon, he tried to drag him on the road. Vishal was resisting to his best, but all his efforts went in vain.

'You will fuck me in my car, no?' the man, having good physique, slapped Vishal again. In between, Nitin came to save him.

'Why are you beating him?' Nitin asked.

'Get out from here,' two men, having the rod in their hand, pushed Nitin as well.

'Bastard! You will fuck me in my car. Bob and Robin, just go and teach them a lesson,' Soon, four men with their equipments rushed to the shop and started to destroy all the stuff.

'*Mummy…mummy* please save us,' Nitin shouted loudly, while other two boys were beating Vishal brutally with their legs and hands. Vishal was crying. Hearing their voices, Savitri and Reena came out of the house. By then, six or seven neighbours had also come out. But, it was too late as the shop had been shattered.

'What did you do, dog? Why are you beating my children?' Savitri gave a slap to that boy, who was beating Vishal, but that "muscleman" shoved her as well. Neighbours turned out to be spectators as if they were watching a movie.

'Reena, call up the police,' Savitri said.

'Come on, guys, sit in car,' all rushed to sit in car hearing Savitri's remark.

'Please, catch them. Don't keep looking like strangers,' Savitri shouted, but people didn't respond. Soon, the boys ran away in the car.

'Oh! Everything has been destroyed,' Nitin said.

'Don't worry, I will take revenge from them,' Vishal replied.

'Reena, you go inside. I am going to the police station to file an F.I.R.,' Savitri said.

'At this time,'

'Yes, at this time. I will show the police what these rich hooligans have done to us.' Savitri spoke firmly.

FORTY

'Hello Dinesh, are you happy now?' Next day, Kapil was talking to Dinesh at his house. Both were drinking in Kapil's room.

'Yes, now, I am happy. The burden of getting slapped by Vishal is over.'

'Hahahaha! It is reflecting on your face,'

'Why not, I couldn't sleep properly for last so many days,'

'But, yesterday, you would have slept well,'

'Yes...but,'

'What?' Kapil became attentive.

'Why did they destroy Nitin's shop?'

'I also felt bad about this. It happened in a misunderstanding,' Kapil said.

'They did absolutely right. I want to hit Nitin from every point, so that he is not in a proper state of mind to play in the trial matches after two months,' Kapil spoke in his mind.

'What are you thinking?' Dinesh asked.

'I am just worried about Nitin. His father is not getting his salary. Now, his small business too....' Kapil pretended.

'That's why I am a little disappointed, Kapil. We had decided to teach a lesson to Vishal, but Nitin had to face all this,' Dinesh said.

'Don't worry. I will help him in the best possible way,' Kapil spoke.

'Yes, we should support him in the best possible way as the month of October has the biggest challenge for Nitin,' Dinesh said.

'Not only Nitin, but for both of us, as well,' Kapil said.

'Yes, I know, but Nitin has a better chance to be selected in India under-nineteen team, as U.P.C.A. and all the national selectors are backing him,' Dinesh said.

'Yes, he has a far better chance,' Kapil said.

'Let me see how he plays in the under-nineteen World Cup?' Kapil spoke in his mind again.

'Where are you lost again?' Dinesh asked.

'Nowhere, I was just thinking how I help Nitin without hurting his self respect.'

'Hmmm… OK. I should move now, bye-bye,' Dinesh got up from the sofa.

'Bye-bye, dear, meet you tomorrow in the ground. Sleep properly. If don't sleep properly, then how will you get selected in the Indian team?' Kapil told Dinesh.

'You have done your job for my good sleep. Bye-bye,' Dinesh smiled.

'Bye-bye.'

Almost after a week after that incident, Nitin was offering his prayers in the morning, in front of his makeshift temple, in a white kit.

Om jai Tendalya hare
Swami Jai Tendalya hare
Team India ke sankat
Sathiyonke tum sankat
Kshan men door kare
Om jai Tendalya hare
Jo dhyawe, Phalpawe
Dukh bin se sabka
Dukh bin se India ka
Ranonkee Barish ho Jawe

Balla jo sur lagawe
Vinash ho dushmanka
Om jai Tendalya hare

'What is this Nitin?' Savitri said as he unfolded his hands and opened his yes. She was observing him closely for last few minutes.

'*Mummy, woooo...*'

'Where did you learn this from?'

'It was prepared by me.'

'You converted (Hindu God) *aarti* (worship) into Tendalya's *aarti.*'

'By the way, since how long have you been doing this?' Savitri asked with surprise.

'It has been very long.'

'You mean that ever since you started the worshipping,'

'No, after two years of that,'

'But why do you worship Jatin?'

'You will not understand, *mummy*. He is not only mine, but has been the God of many cricketers. Many people worship him in India.'

'*Ufff*! I am not able to understand. By the way, is your match today?'

'No, mom. Actually, Ranji Trophy camp is starting from today. Next month, the first two Ranji Trophy matches are going to take place for the selection of India under-nineteen team for the World Cup.'

'Oh! But why are you looking so tensed and disappointed?'

'You already know, *mummy*. The shop has been shut down ever since that fight took place. Stuff worth fifty thousand rupees has been ruined, Nitin became weepy.

'I am also worried. There is someone around, who is not happy with our progress. By the way, you need not worry about that. I have found a solution for you.'

'What?' Nitin asked.

'Reena......Reena,' Savitri called out.

'Yes, *mummy,'* Reema came out quickly from the kitchen.

'Bring jewellery from the safe.'

What will you do with the jewellery, *mummy*?' Nitin intervened with surprise.

'I will take loan on it. I have already spoken to a goldsmith. You can start the shop again,' Savitri said.

'But, this jewellery is for Reena *di*'s marriage.'

'Don't worry, Nitin. My first priority is earning. We have to set up the shop again. God willing, we will make more jewellery like this,' Reena supported him.

'Thank you, *di,'* tears started rolling down Nitin's cheeks.

'Don't take tension and just focus on your game. Everyone is looking up to you. Everybody wants you to be selected in the India under-nineteen team,' Reena spoke.

'Yes, *di*, I will put my best foot forward,' Nitin assured.

'Now, you should move to the ground.'

'Oh yes, I am getting late,' Nitin said looking at his wrist watch. He immediately came into action.

'Hey, have you eaten your breakfast?' Reena asked.

'No, I am getting late. I will purchase fruits on my way.'

'We will also come with you as I have to meet the goldsmith,' Savitri said.

'OK, no problem,' soon, the trio left the house.

FORTY ONE

Bhagwan ho tum cricket ke
SharanGahu mainkiski
SharanGahu mainkiski
Tum Bin Aurnaduja
Tum Bin Aurnaduja
AasKaru main kiski
Om jai tedalya hare

Nitin was offering prayers in the morning at around 7:30 a.m., in front of his makeshift temple. He worshipped his kit-bag and bat, as well. A small photo of Jatin Tendulkar was stuck on his bat along with his autograph.

'Is the prayers over?' Savitri entered the room with a glass of milk and breakfast.

'Yes, *mummy*,'

'Then, eat your breakfast properly,' Savitri dragged the small table and put all the stuff on that.

'Reena *di*, Shalu hasn't come as yet,' Nitin said while drinking the milk.

'I called her just few minutes back. She is about to reach. Look, she has reached,' Reena replied seeing outside.

'Hey, Nitin, Good morning,' Shalu said.

'Good morning,' Nitin replied.

'Are you done with your breakfast?' Savitri asked.

'No, actually I got up late. So, I have to rush immediately.'

'You both talk. I will prepare breakfast for you,' Savitri told Reena and Shalu.

'Thanks, aunty,' Shalu spoke.

'So, what's up? Are you ready? *Di* will go with you,' Nitin spoke to Shalu.

'Sorry, Nitin. Actually, *papa* had to go somewhere early this morning. So, I couldn't bring the car.'

'Then, how will you reach the ground?' Nitin asked.

'I have told *papa* about this. He will come back at around eleven. I will reach by the lunch time.' Shalu said.

'Then, what will you do *di*?' Nitin looked towards his sister.

'Don't worry. I will wait and come along with her during lunch time.' Reena said.

'OK, Shalu, you pick up Reena *di* as well,' Nitin told Shalu.

'Don't worry, I will,' Shalu smiled.

'Hey, Shalu, eat your breakfast,' Savitri entered the room.

'OK, *mummy*, I should move now,' Nitin got up from the bed.

'But, why are you looking so tense?' Savitri asked.

'Yes, *mummy*, I am little nervous. It is going to be the biggest test, so far,' Nitin replied.

'Don't worry, my son. Our blessings are with you,' Savitri said, hugging him.

'Yes, my brother, I have full confidence in you. You will rock in the next four days,' Reena caught Nitin's hand.

'And, me, too,' Shalu put her neck on Nitin's shoulder.

'Hey, Reena, just pick up the vermillion's case,' Savitri pointed towards the worship plate.

'My blessings are always with you, my son,' Savitri said while putting vermillion on Nitin's forehead.

'OK, *mummy*, I should move finally.' Nitin touched his mother's feet and sister's, too.

'How will you go?' Shalu asked.

'By rickshaw,' Nitin replied.

'Why don't you go with Kapil Tiwari? I will just call him.' Shalu started to push the button of her mobile.

'Yes, that's a good idea,' Nitin spoke.

'I have spoken to Kapil Tiwari. He will come with his family and few relatives,' Shalu informed.

'Then, you should move. It is already 8 o'clock,' Savitri said.

'What time will the match start?' Reena asked.

'At 9:30 a.m. OK, bye-bye,' Nitin picked up his kit-bag and walked towards the gate. Everyone came with him till the gate.

'Hey, brother, please stop,' Nitin said as he passed by Shalu's house.

'What happened?' the rickshaw-puller asked after stopping.

'Yes, there is my friend,' Nitin kept looking at the other side for a while.

'Why did Shalu tell a lie to me? Her father is reading the newspaper and the car is also in the house,' Nitin said in a low tone while thinking seriously.

'Is there any problem?'

'No, you should move,' as he ordered, the rickshaw puller started to move ahead but, Nitin was completely in a thinking mode.

'Move fast, brother,' Nitin spoke.

'Sir, I didn't eat breakfast, that's why I am a bit slow,' the rickshaw-puller paced up a bit. He didn't know that he was going to see the worst day of his life in a little while.

FORTY TWO

'*Ya allah...ya allah* (Oh God),' almost after ten minutes, both, Nitin and the rickshaw-puller, were lying on the road, crying, as a speeding car had hit the rickshaw badly. Both were bleeding. Nitin's trousers were worn out at the bottom and there was a big cut below his knee. Rickshaw-puller was bleeding on his face. Almost twenty to thirty people gathered around them. All were talking to each other but the car had hit and run.

'Are you going to play Ranji Trophy match?' one person from the crowd asked. Nitin only nodded while moaning. He was in tears and the same condition was that of the rickshaw-puller.

'Hey, talk to him later. First we should take them to a doctor. They need first-aid badly,' the other person replied.

'Call for two rickshaws immediately,' someone from the crowd said. Soon, Nitin and the rickshaw-puller were sitting in separate rickshaws. As soon as the rickshaw-puller started to move, a loud voice forced them to stop.

'Hey, Nitin, what happened, my son?' Deepak Khandekar, coach of the Green Park hostel, stopped his bike and rushed to catch Nitin.

'What happened, my son?' Khandekar replaced the man, who was supporting Nitin on the rickshaw.

'Sir, a speeding car hit us badly from the side,' Nitin said.

'Your leg is bleeding badly. Does anyone have a bandage?' Khandekar shouted.

'Sir, please take this and wrap on the wound,' one person said, giving a big hanky to him.

'Please help me to make him sit on my bike and you, make him sit on yours,' Khandekar said to a person, who didn't object.

'Sir, my kit-bag,' Nitin said.

'Where is the kit-bag?'

'Sir, it also fell on the road, when the rickshaw toppled,' Nitin said.

'Look out friends, there will be a kit-bag around,' Khandekar said to the people in a loud voice. People scattered and started to look around. Some of them walked away for a few metres towards either side, but they didn't find the kit-bag'.

'Sir, we didn't find the kit-bag. It seems that the kit-bag has been stolen,' a man replied. Nitin broke down badly.

'Don't cry, my son. Let it be stolen. I will give you a new kit-bag.' Khandekar ordered a man to make Nitin sit on the bike. Soon, three to four men helped Nitin to sit on the bike.

'You also sit behind him,' Khandekar said to one person. As both of them sat, Khandekar paced up his bike. Soon, both the bikes were heading towards the hospital. One was carrying Nitin and the other one, the rickshaw-puller.

* * *

'There has been a huge problem, sir,' U.P. captain, Narendra Pandey said to the coach, Satpal Sharma as he returned to the pavilion after the toss.

'What happened?' the coach asked with a tensed face.

'Sir, the railway has won the toss and elected to bat first.'

'Then, what?'

'Sir, you know that Nitin has been injured badly. How will he field?'

'You need not worry, sir. I will field,' Nitin intervened as he was listening to the conversation.

'But, how will you? You have a serious injury. How will you run on the ground? Why do you want to take a risk. Rules have allowed us to go in with an extra fielder since very first ball.'

'No problem, I will field, let it pain. If the leg bleeds, then I will see later. You know how important this match is for me,' Nitin said.

'Let him do the fielding, sir. He is very strong,' Kapil said, staring at Nitin's injury. His gaze was telling a lot.

'OK. If you face any serious problem and the U.P.C.A. asks any questions from me, then you will have to take the responsibility,' Coach Satpal Sharma replied by putting hand on his shoulder.

'No problem, sir.'

'Go ahead, my boy, and fight,' captain Narendra said.

'Thanks a lot, sir,' Nitin said.

FORTY THREE

'There is no need to cry, my boy, don't cry. Everything will be OK.' Savitri got up and hugged Nitin who was weeping loudly.

'No, *mom*, at least in this match, nothing good will happen,' Nitin spoke.

'Why will it not happen?Two days are still left in the game,' Reena said.

'It's very-very difficult *di*. We have already taken the lead of almost two hundred and fifty runs. We still have five wickets in hand,' Nitin spoke.

'What does that mean?' Savitri asked with curiosity.

'It means that Nitin's team, much likely, will not be required to bat again to win this match,' Reena replied.

'And, even if the team gets to bat again and, I am promoted from number five to the opening position, then we will hardly have sufficient score to chase,' Nitin said, sobbing.

'Oh,' Savitri became serious.

'You, my friends and people from the colony came to see me making a big score but, I could face only two balls,' Nitin broke down again after saying that.

'Don't weep, brother. Whatever has to happen, always happens,' Reena said.

'Yes, you are absolutely right *di*,' Shalu entered the room at the same time.

'Why are you crying like a child?' Shalu spoke.

'It's a matter of my life, Shalu. My selection for the World Cup is at stake,' Nitin replied.

'But what is the advantage of crying for failure, since nothing can be done right now,' Shalu said.

'I am also a human being. I also feel pain because of failure,' Nitin looked towards her and spoke in a weepy voice.

'By the way, what's the status of your injury?' Shalu asked.

'It has healed a lot in the last two days. Now he has less pain compared to the first day,' Reena replied instead of Nitin.

'Yes, I got enough time to rest as the railway was bundled out only at 119 in the first innings,' Nitin said. It has been 9.00 p.m.,' Reena reminded him.

'Oh yes, I will have to rush to the hotel,' Nitin said, wiping out his tears, and got up.

'Don't think about the past and look ahead,' Savitri hugged him.

'Hmmmm,' Nitin just nodded.

FORTY FOUR

'Hey, you rocked, Kapil Tiwari! You rocked,' Shalu was talking to Kapil through her mobile while lying on her bed, early in the morning.

'Thanks, Shalu,' Kapil responded from the other side.

'Today, when I opened the sports page and saw your photo, the headlines grabbed my attention: 'Kapil stakes his claim for India under-nineteen team with a solid "Man of the Match" ton,' Shalu read the headlines of a leading newspaper.

'Thank you very much, madam. It is an honour for me that you gave importance to my news,' Kapil spoke.

'No, my dear, the entire locality and U.P., I should say, is rejoicing.'

'Oh, Really! Whole U.P.?'

'Why not? After all, after so many years, a U.P. boy has staked claim for India under-nineteen team, though I have a feeling that you have already been selected.'

'May your words turn out to be true,' Kapil spoke.

'They will, Kapil Tiwari. My prediction always turns out to be true. It's my inner voice.'

'Let's see what happens this time,'

'You really did a wonderful job. All were expecting from Nitin but, you changed the whole picture,' Shalu said.

'Thank you,'

'Thanks is not enough,'

'Then, what?'

'There should be a grand party,'

'Sure, I will give a grand party. Let the second match finish and officials announce the Indian under-nineteen team for the World Cup.

'No, you will have to throw a party soon. This party will be for your becoming the man of the match. For the selection, there must be a special party,' spoke Shalu.

'OK, dear, OK.'

'Then, I should invite Nitin and the entire group,' Shalu said.

'Not Nitin,'

'But, why should we not invite him?' Shalu asked.

'You know he couldn't even open his account while everyone was expecting so much from him. It wouldn't be right to celebrate in his presence as that would not make him feel good,' Kapil pretended.

'Hmmm, you are absolutely right' Shalu agreed.

'This party will be especially for you, Shalu. And there will be no other person. Please come to my house day after tomorrow. First we will celebrate and then go on a long drive again.' Kapil offered.

'Sure, I will come. This is for your fantastic ton. OK. Bye-bye.'

'Bye, dear.' Kapil disconnected the phone.

'Hi, are you waiting for me?' Shalu waved her hand from almost ten metres as she saw Kapil standing outside the gate.

'Yes, dear. I am waiting for you,'

'Wow! Your bungalow is glowing. It seems that you have made a special arrangement,' Shalu said with a surprise as the bungalow, which was decorated with flowers and fur below, took her attention.

'It has been done for you, darling. You are looking beautiful today,'

'Hey, liar,'

'Believe me,'

'It's OK. Shall we move inside?' Shalu smiled at Kapil.

'Oh yes, I was completely lost in your beauty. Today, you are looking absolutely stunning.' Both started to walk inside the bungalow.

Kapil kept praising her till they stepped into the first room. Shalu was looking beautiful in black mini-skirt with pink top.

'Why is there so silence in Bungalow? No one is being seen except for the servants. Where are uncle and aunty?' Shalu asked.

'*Papa* is busy in the arrangements for the next match. You know that he is the chairman of the Kanpur Cricket Association, as well.' Kapil spoke.

'And, aunty?' Shalu asked.

'She has gone to my uncle's house,' Kapil replied.

'Wow! What a fantastic look! You changed your room completely,' Shalu observed the room closely.

'Yes, I changed again according to your wish' Kapil said.

'Yes, the room is full of pink colour. There is a pink bed sheet, pink cups, pink shoes, and even tab of spout has been converted into pink colour,' Shalu spoke in excitement.

'You have made my life pink as well,' Kapil spoke in a romantic tone.

'By the way, take a seat and tell me what will you like to have? Something cold or hot?' Kapil asked Shalu.

'Cold drink, and that too a special one,' Shalu replied.

'Black Label,'

'Yes,' Shalu blinked at him while reading a book. Kapil picked up the cordless phone and ordered. Soon, a servant came in with a big tray, which had one bottle, and some other stuff.

'Take your peg,' he offered the peg and sat beside her on a huge sofa.

'Cheers! Let's start the celebration.' Both started to drink.

'Tell me what's going on?' Kapil said.

'As usual, fitness in the morning and it has been long since I went to the college. In evenings, I am busy in dance class. I am also waiting for your second Ranji Trophy and the final trial match.' Shalu spoke.

'Hmmm, but for a very long time, I have been waiting for you. Today, you are looking stunning,' Kapil kissed on her cheek. It left Shalu blushing.

'How are your preparations for the second match going on?' Shalu asked after taking a sip.

'The ton has given me enough confidence. Our camp will start after two days,' Kapil replied.

'Hmmm, I am praying for your another ton,'

'For Nitin, as well,' as Kapil said that, Shalu coughed three times.

'Hey, what happened?'

'Nothing...nothing,'

'Are you OK?'

'Yes, I am fine. By the way, what were you saying?'

'I was asking about Nitin,'

'Yes, I am praying for both of you. I always pray for both of you. May you both be selected in Indian under-nineteen!' Shalu said.

'Just leave cricket now. Please come in my lap,' Kapil caught her hand and took her close to himself by little force.

'Hey what are you doing? Look at that' Shalu pointed out.

'Oh,' Kapil got up and closed the door.

'Please, come,' Kapil extended his hand to her. Shalu got up and sat in his lap. Kapil started to kiss on her neck and cheek. As Shalu loosened her body, he took his hand to her b***s. He turned her towards his face and started to suck her lips. Shalu, too, was in a mood and responding equally. Within minutes, Kapil took her skirt and top, off her body and started kissing on her thigh and the entire body, passionately.

Black Label and Kapil's lips had made her far intoxicated. He took her into his lap and lay down on the bed. Her tight and very fair body was glittering in black bra and panty. Kapil took his shirt and pants off. He was only in shorts. He lay down beside her and started to suck her lips. Soon, he unhooked her bra as well and Shalu, didn't object. Kapil started to suck her b***s and his hands were playing with her lower portion. Within minutes, he took the black panty off her body and his shorts as well. Both of them were completely nude and kissing each other passionately, turning sides. The entire room was savouring with expensive perfume and warm breaths. That play kept on going for almost fifteen minutes. Finally, Kapil put her at rest and penetrated his part into her body.

'Kapil, please,' Shalu almost cried. He put his hand on her lips and started to push his lower portion frequently with more power. After the final dig, he lay on her body. Both tightly embraced each other and were breathing heavily. After five minutes, Kapil turned his neck back and gazed at his big picture was fitted on the wall in designing frame. He gave a smile to his picture, which was smiling back.

FORTY FIVE

Tum ho ranonke Sagar
Ballebajonke swami
Swami Tum sankathari
Beda paarkaro tum
Beda paarkaro tum
O Sankathari
Om Jai Tendalya hare

After a week, not only Nitin, but all the family members, including Shalu were offering prayers in front of the small makeshift temple. The difference was that Nitin was humming Tendalya's *aarti*, while the remaining were singing Ganesh *Ji*'s. All, except Shalu, seemed to be tensed and sad. Savitri broke the silence as the worship was over.

'Take the blessings of God. Now, only God can do something for you,' Savitri forwarded the plate of worship towards Nitin.

'Yes, *mummy*, you are right. My life is almost over,' Nitin replied in a weepy voice.

'Don't worry, my son. This is not the end of the world. 'Perhaps God wants something better for you that's why it has been happening for last three days.' As Savitri hugged Nitin, he broke down.

'Don't weep, my son, everything will be OK,' Savitri spoke again.

'Yes Nitin, you are extraordinary talented and have potential. There is no need to be worried,' Shalu showed her sympathy by putting her hand on his shoulder.

'How will it be fine, how? Last three days have been completely wiped out by rain. Why are you giving me false assurance?' Nitin shouted.

'First, stop crying and go to the hotel immediately as your team meeting is about to start,' Reena intervened.

'OK, *di,'* Nitin said by wiping out his tears.

'OK, *mummy*, I should move now,' Nitin said.

'Don't be tensed and take care of yourself,' Savitri said as Nitin touched her feet. Nitin moved outside.

'Stop for a while, I am also coming,' Shalu said and both started walking together.

'Shalu, will you come with me to the team hotel?' Nitin asked as both passed in front of the park.

'It's tough for me, Nitin. You know all members of the team will be there. I hope you can understand,' Shalu said.

'Do you have any problem in sitting in the park for few minutes?'

'Not at all. We will sit at the back side as there is dark and no light.' Soon, they were sitting on the bench, in one corner of the park.

'Shalu, I am feeling very lonely and suffocated today,' Nitin said. His head was in her lap and he was rubbing her hand.

'Don't worry, Nitin. The under-nineteen World Cup is not a matter of life or death,' Shalu said.

'It is, Shalu, it is. You don't realise the importance of under-nineteen World Cup. Good performance in this tournament will make my journey to team India, far easy. Take the examples of Kaif and Yuvraj,' Nitin said in a weepy voice.

'That's OK but what can be done now?' Shalu said.

'I will not be able to survive, if I am not selected in the team,' Nitin spoke.

'Don't talk like that. I am always with you,' having said that, Shalu bent her face down and started kissing on his lips. Nitin, too, embraced her tightly.

FORTY SIX

A small party was going on at Kapil's house, in which Kapil Tiwari, his close friends, relatives and his father's friends were invited, including Shalu. It was around 10:30 p.m.

'Ha-ha-ha..., Cheers, my son and Congratulations! No one can stop you from getting selected in India under-nineteen team,' Dharmendra Tiwari said. 'Yes, *papa*. Tomorrow or day after, the team would be announced for the World Cup,' Kapil spoke.

'Yes, Kapil Tiwari, your selection is pretty much on the cards. Since, three days have already been washed out and tomorrow is the last day and, rain is forecasted even for tomorrow,' one of his relatives said.

'What about future Tendulkar?' a relative asked further. This question was followed by a burst of laughter. But, the strange thing was that Shalu, too, was a part of it.

'Hey, he is the future Tendulkar. Do you know Sharma *ji* that Tendulkar, also never played the under-nineteen World Cup? So, the future Tendulkar is also not required to play in the same to qualify for the senior team,' Kapil's father, Dharmendra Tiwari, made a sarcastic remark in response.

'You are absolutely right, Dharmendra *ji*. Ha-ha-ha-ha,' the sound of laughter echoed again.

'By the way, Tiwari *ji*, have all the arrangements for the prize distribution been done?'

'Yes, everythig is done,'

'At what time will the Chief Minister reach?'

'Even if tomorrow's play is washed out, he will come at 5:30 p.m.'

'OK, sir, plz allow me. I have to reach the ground, early morning. And, many-many congratulations to your son again,' Sharma said.

'Thank you, Sharma *ji*.'

'Hey, Kapil Tiwari, I am very happy for you,' Dinesh entered the hall and hugged Kapil Tiwari.

'Why did you get late, my dear?'

'My car was giving some problem so, I had to call the mechanic.'

'It's OK.'

'By the way, where is your darling?'

'She is talking with mom in the first room,' Kapil replied.

'Actually I had to tell you something about her,' Dinesh said.

'Hmm…go ahead,' Kapil said.

'You will not mind, right?'

'Don't worry, dear, go ahead,' Kapil spoke.

'Actually, there was a problem in my car in front of the Gandhi Park,'

'OK, then what?'

'I saw Shalu and Nitin coming out of the park, together,' Dinesh spoke.

'What,'

'Are you sure they were Nitin and Shalu?' Kapil asked with curiosity.

'Yes, dear. I am not blind,' Dinesh answered.

'What time it would have been?'

'Around 9:00 p.m.'

'Hmmm, he didn't even come for the team meeting,' Kapil said, recalling.

'I think she is playing a double game,' Dinesh said.

'But, I have already played the game with her,' Kapil said.

'What game?' Dinesh asked.

'You will have to wait. Let the team be announced,' Kapil winked at him.

'OK'.

FORTY SEVEN

Next day, the Green Park ground was almost full. Some players from both the teams were playing football in a corner, some were chatting in groups and, officials, too, were busy in discussions. Kapil's father was heading towards the umpires, who were busy inspecting the pitch.

'How is the pitch, sir? Is it still wet?' Tiwari asked as he reached close to them.

We are inspecting, Tiwari *ji*. After consulting the match referee, we will let you know in next fifteen minutes,' one umpire replied.

'It's OK, sir. No problem.'

* * *

'The match will be played, but it will be for fifty overs,' after fifteen minutes, the match referee announced, in presence of the team captain, coaches and managers.

'What! How is it possible? Captains of both the team spoke together with surprise.

'We got this order from Board of Cricket Control for India (B.C.C.I.) just five minutes back,' the match referee said.

'There must be solid reason behind it, sir. It never happened in the history of Ranji Trophy ,' the coach of U.P. Ranji team intervened.

'At least six players from both the teams are on trial for the under-nineteen World Cup. All the players are very important. They are the stars. It is only match of domestic session which three days have been washed out. B.C.C.I. has set tomorrow evening as the deadline to announce under-19 for the world cup team. It has already taken ten extra days. So, this is a special arrangement,' the match referee stood up from the chair and said loudly.

'But, sir, rule doesn't allow,' Dharmendra Tiwari intervened who was listening all with lot of attention.

'Both teams will be compensated from different points of view. I have no time. Be ready in fifteen minutes to play a fifty over match,' saying this, the match referee came out of the room. It left the captains of both the teams and officials silent. They also came out of the room.

'Guys, it will be a fifty over match as per the order of B.C.C.I. So, be ready and put on your kits,' as the U.P. captain announced this in the dressing room, Nitin's face got lit-up with a smile. He thanked God by taking his hands up and kissed on his locket many times, which was having Tendulkar's picture.

* * *

After one day, Nitin was dancing on the tune of D.J. in his park, which was arranged by the people of his locality. Everybody was dancing and it was an electrifying atmosphere. Shalu, too, was involved among the dancers, including his sister, Reena and friends. But, neither Kapil nor Dinesh was involved despite being invited.

'Nitin is the next Tendulkar. My brother is the next Tendulkar,' Vishal spoke loudly while dancing and took Nitin on his shoulder. Beer was having its impact.

'Yes, yes, 'Reena was also dancing in a corner with Shalu. In between, Vishal picked-up the newspaper and started reading the headlines: "Nitin's ton sunk the railway. Nitin is the only player to be selected in India under-nineteen team for the World Cup from Uttar Pradesh" Vishal was dancing and reading it again and again. Celebration was at its best. Suddenly, Shalu stopped dancing.

'Hey, why did you stop?' Reena said.

'My mobile has been buzzing for long. I didn't realise that in this noise and frolic of dance,' Shalu replied.

'You wouldn't be able to listen here. Just go out of the park' Reena advised her.

'Yes, *di*, you are right,' Shalu came out of the park.

'Kapil, where have you been?' Shalu spoke after receiving the call.

'Where should I be at this time?' Kapil replied.

'Why didn't you come here?' Shalu asked.

'Do you think it would be right for me to come over there?' Kapil said.

'Why not?' Shalu said.

'It means that I did a mistake by not inviting Nitin when I threw the party after my hundred, no? I am not selected Shalu.'

'Actually, had you been here, I would have felt nice,' Shalu replied after a pause of almost thirty seconds.

'Shalu, you are a master in changing the topic,'

'I didn't understand that,' Shalu spoke.

'I don't know whether you understand or……by the way, can you come immediately to my house as I am feeling very lonely,' Kapil cut his sentence short and changed the topic.

'Yes, I will try my level best,' Shalu replied.

'OK then, I am waiting,' having said that Kapil disconnected the phone.

'Whose call it was?' Reena asked as Shalu reached inside.

'*Papa* was calling,' Shalu told a lie to Reena.

'OK, come and dance now.' Reena told Shalu.

Shalu became busy in dancing again. During this, her mobile kept buzzing at regular intervals, but she didn't receive the call.

'Why didn't you take my call, Shalu?' Kapil shouted through his mobile the next morning.

'I had put the mobile on silent mode,' Shalu said.

'You are telling a lie,' Kapil spoke.

'You can think whatever you want to,' Shalu said.

'I waited for you yesterday till 11.00 p.m.'

'Actually, I was caught up in a strange situation. My friends didn't allow me to leave,' Shalu spoke.

'Friends didn't allow or you didn't want to come,' Kapil said changing his tone.

'You are free to think your own way,' Shalu spoke.

'Shalu, I desperately needed you yesterday. How will you support me in the rest of my life?'

'Rest of the life, what do you mean?' Shalu said.

'What will you do after marriage?' Kapil told.

'Marriage,' she said in a tone of surprise.

'Why are you so surprised?' Kapil asked.

'How did marriage come in between?' Shalu asked.

'Why will it not come? You are my girlfriend? How unlucky I am, instead of reducing my pain, you were celebrating my arch rival's success,' Kapil spoke in bitterness. Shalu didn't respond.

'All my guesses are turning out to be true,' Kapil said.

'What guesses?' Shalu spoke.

'Just leave it now. I will talk to you about this some other day.' Kapil disconnected the call.

FORTY EIGHT

'Fuck off, all my efforts went in vain.' Kapil threw the bat on the floor in anger, while walking in his hall.

'It has been because of the B.C.C.I. Even the rain subterfuged us on the last day,' Dinesh said.

'Finally that peon's son has peed on our face,' Kapil turned up to Dinesh.

'Don't worry, dear. You have many Ranji Trophy matches. You can stake your claim for Duleep or Irani Trophy,' Dinesh said.

'I have been humiliated a lot. People are laughing at us,' Kapil spoke in anger.

'Don't pay attention to that, Kapil Tiwari. The more you think about this, more upset you will be,' Dinesh consoled him.

'I wish some miracle would happen. If Nitin were injured, I would have replaced him as I am the first standby for the World Cup,' Kapil said.

'When is the team going on the Bangladesh tour?' Dinesh asked.

'Team will leave for Bangladesh after four days. All the players will assemble in Hotel Taj in Mumbai two days before the team departs,' Kapil said.

'By the way, you were absolutely right, Dinesh,' Kapil said.

'What?'

'She is playing a double game,' Kapil spoke.

'Are you hundred per cent sure?' Dinesh said.

'Yes, I have cross-checked. My doubt is absolutely clear now. By the way, I want to show you something,' Kapil said.

'What?'

'Look at this,' Kapil took out his costly mobile and showed it to Dinesh. As the time passed, Dinesh's eyes kept widening.

'Oh my God! When did you do that?' Dinesh took his eyes off the mobile after almost ten minutes.

'Just few days back,' Kapil replied.

'Sir is calling you in his room,' suddenly, a servant intervened.

'You sit here, I am coming in five minutes,' Kapil told Dinesh.

'No problem.' Dinesh picked up the Cricket Samrat magazine (a known Hindi magazine on cricket) from a table and started reading it. After five minutes, Kapil returned.

'What happened?' Dinesh asked.

'Actually, I got a call from the B.C.C.I. office,' Kapil said after sitting beside Dinesh.

'When?'

'Just ten minutes back, on dad's mobile,' Kapil spoke.

'What's the matter?' Dinesh put the book back on the table.

'They have asked me to reach Hotel Taj, Mumbai after two days,' Kapil replied.

'Congratulations, perhaps you have been selected,' Dinesh spoke.

'It's difficult to predict as the B.C.C.I. spokesman didn't say anything clearly,' Kapil shrugged his shoulder.

'It means you will have to leave for Mumbai tomorrow,' Dinesh said.

'Yes, in the evening,'

'OK, you must wait then. By the way, I should move now. I am getting late,' Dinesh said

'OK, but there is request for you,' Kapil said.

'What?'

'Please don't discuss this B.C.C.I. matter with anyone. I told you because you are my best friend and I share thick and thin with you,' Kapil said.

'Come on, no problem, you are a darling,' Dinesh said.

'OK, bye-bye,'

'Bye-bye,' Kapil hugged Dinesh. He left the hall and walked towards the gate of the bungalow. After walking for about hundred metres, he returned to the building.

'Yes, what happened?' Kapil asked as he opened the door of the hall.

'The old problem,' Dinesh gave the mobile to him.

'Oh, it happened again!' Kapil replied, laughing loudly.

'Wait for a minute.' Kapil went inside. He came at the gate with his mobile and exchanged with Dinesh.

'I think we must change our mobile phones. Since we have the same models, both have been interchanged countless times,' Dinesh said.

'Yes, you are absolutely right. I am also fed up of this. I will purchase another model soon,' Kapil said.

'OK, take care. When you reach Mumbai, inform me on the matter,' Dinesh said.

'Ok, bye,' having said that, Kapil closed the door and Dinesh walked towards the gate again.

FORTY NINE

Tum ho Prahaarke Swami
Bowleron men Bhayabharta
Swami bowleron men BhayaBharta
Men Adnasakhiladi
Men sewak, tum swami
KripaKaroBharta
Om jai Tendalya Hare

Like always, before leaving for Mumbai, Nitin was doing "worship" in his room, while his fast friend Vishal, sister, mother and Shalu, were humming the traditional *aarti*. As the *aarti* got over, Nitin picked up his kit-bag and the box of clothes.

'Have you checked all your stuff?' Savitri asked.

'There is no need to be worried, mom, I have checked everything thrice,' Reena replied.

'Touch your father's feet as well,' Savitri said. As she ordered, Nitin entered the small room-cum-store, which was adjacent to the last room. He was in tears. He touched Seetaram's feet whose tears were rolling down the cheeks as well.

'*Mummy*, look after *papa*, give him a massage daily,' Nitin spoke.

'Who does it in your absence?' Savitri remarked.

'I am just reminding you,' Nitin said.

'Don't worry about that son and you should move now.' As everyone came out, around fifty people from the colony, greeted him, standing around the parked car.

"Best wishes my son"..."You have to bring the under-nineteen World Cup along with you"..."You have to make at least two hundred runs in the tournament". As many people were there, so many comments and wishes were floating around. Nitin responded to them either by touching their feet, saying thanks, or kissing on the cheeks of the children. After fifteen minutes or so, Nitin sat in the car with Vishal, mother and sister. The car caught up speed towards the railway station to catch the train for Lucknow, from where he had to catch a flight to Mumbai.

FIFTY

'Hey, Kapil you are here. Am I seeing a dream?' Nitin said with surprise as he saw Kapil Tiwari in the lobby of Hotel Taj.

'No, you are not seeing a dream,' Kapil replied.

'But,'

'Just four days back, I was instructed by the B.C.C.I. to come over here,' Kapil spoke.

Kapil reply made Nitin worried and suspicious.

'When did you come?' Nitin asked Kapil Tiwari.

'This morning,' Kapil replied.

'OK, have all the players come?' Nitin asked.

'They are coming in at regular intervals,' Kapil replied.

'OK, come with me to my room,' Nitin said, and Kapil followed him.

'At what time do we have to assemble?' Kapil asked while putting his bags in the room.

'After one hour, we have to assemble in Vinod Mathur sir's room,' Nitin replied.

'Is he our manager?' Kapil asked.

'Yes,'

'Nice, he is a nice man,'

'OK, let me sleep for sometime as I am feeling tired. If you want to sleep here, it is your wish,' Nitin spoke.

'No, I am going out. I have to purchase T-shirts from the Colaba market,' Kapil said.

'Please wake me up when the meeting starts,' Nitin lay on the bed.

* * *

'Good evening, sir. How are you, sir?' Nitin said as he opened the door. The manager of under-nineteen team, Vinod Mathur, woke him up by knocking at the door.

'I am fine, Nitin. Can I come inside?' Mathur asked.

'Yes sir, why not?' Nitin made way for him.

'Nitin, I have come here to meet you and have a special talk,' Mathur said, sitting in a chair.

'Is it an important matter, sir?' Nitin asked.

'Yes, very important. Sit down please. Do you remember your date of birth on the passport?' Mathur looked into Nitin's eyes.

'No, sir, it was made long time back by my parents.' Mathur's question turned Nitin's face absolutely serious.

'And, your tenth certificate?' Mathur asked.

'Sure, sir,' Nitin replied.

'Nitin, let me tell you that your passport is showing you one year overage,' Mathur spoke.

'How can it be, sir? Last year I went to Sri Lanka with under-nineteen team on the same passport,' Nitin spoke with agitation.

'At that time, you were under-nineteen according to your passport,'

'But, sir…'

'Yesterday only, B.C.C.I. got a mail from the tournament organising committee that you are over age by one year,' Mathur informed.

What! Nitin's face turned pale and he became weepy.

'That's why B.C.C.I. has called Kapil here as he was the first standby,' Mathur said.

'Does it mean that I am out of the team?' Nitin asked.

'Yes, Nitin, I am very sorry,' as Mathur said that, Nitin broke down. Mathur kept looking at him with a sad face.

'But, there is small ray of hope for you,' Mathur spoke again.

'What?' Nitin uncovered his face by taking his hands off. His eyes were red.

'Team will leave for Bangladesh in the evening, day after tomorrow. If you can correct your age on the passport by then, matter can be resolved. You have one and a half day for doing this,' Mathur said.

'How can it be done?' Nitin asked.

'You will have to go to the passport office?'

'Where is it?'

'You are from Kanpur, right?'

'Yes, sir,' Nitin answered, sobbing.

'You will have to go to Bareilly. Do you have money,' Mathur asked.

Nitin gave a nod.

'I know somebody in the airlines. I can make arrangements for your flight to Delhi at the earliest from Delhi you can go by either train or bus. Believe me, if your age is rectified on the passport, I assure you that you will be going with the team,' Mathur said with confidence.

'Thanks, sir, please arrange for the tickets. I will go to Bareilly. It's a matter of my life,' Nitin said, wiping out his tears.

FIFTY ONE

'Hello, Shalu. How are you?' Kapil asked as he received the call.

'Where are you, Kapil?' Shalu said in a tired and weepy voice.

'I am walking with my under-nineteen teammates by seaside. It is a fantastic view here! I wish you were here with me. But, what happened to your voice, darling?' Kapil asked.

'You have changed my life, Kapil,' Shalu spoke from the other side on phone.

'What happened, darling?'

'Why did you do that, Kapil?' Shalu broke down.

'What happened, Shalu? Why are you crying?' Kapil walked a little away from his teammates and asked Shalu.

'You have destroyed everything, my honour, self-respect, the respect of my family, and my life, Kapil,' she said crying out loudly.

'But, tell me, after all what have I done?' Kapil spoke.

'I am surprised that you are still talking as if you don't know anything,' Shalu said.

'Really, Shalu, I don't know what you are talking about,' Kapil stressed.

'In case you have forgotten, see your message box and the MMS that you have saved in my name.' There was no response from Kapil's side for a minute. His face turned pale.

'Why are you silent, Kapil?'

'Shalu, I didn't do anything,' he replied in a shaky voice.

'This clip has been shot in your room, Kapil,' Shalu spoke.

'Shalu I am very sorry,' Kapil also started crying.

'Why are you crying, Kapil? The entire Kanpur is watching this MMS. It will be seen by the entire country tomorrow. What should I do, Kapil? What should my parents do?' Shalu was crying.

'Shalu, it's true that I shot it. Yes, it is true that I wanted to take revenge, because you slapped me long time back in a party in front of my friends. Yes, it is true that I was jealous because, despite all my attempts, you were still in love with Nitin. But, I didn't send it to anyone,' Kapil defended himself in a weepy voice.

'You are still telling a lie, Kapil,' Shalu spoke.

'Believe me, Shalu,' Kapil repeated.

'How should I believe in you? What will happen even if I believe? Will this MMS stop circulating if I believed in you?' Kapil didn't answer.

'I have lost everything, Kapil Tiwari. I don't know what will happen tomorrow? But, one thing is clear that I will not spare you at any cost,' having said that, Shalu disconnected the call.

FIFTY TWO

'Hmmm, your matter is very serious,' a middle aged man said to Nitin after inspecting his documents. He was staring closely at Nitin, who sat in front of him, in the passport office in Bareilly.

'Sir, please do something. It is a matter of my life,' Nitin said. My career depends on you, sir,' Nitin pleaded.

'Come closer and sit here,' the middle aged man offered a seat to Nitin and pointed towards him to sit closer to himself rather than sitting in front. Nitin stood up and sat on the seat.

'How much amount can you spend?' the man whispered into Nitin's ears. Nitin didn't respond except for looking into his eyes.

'You will have to spend twenty thousand,' he whispered into his ear again.

'But sir,'

'Not less than twenty thousand,' he said that again.

'OK, sir, you do your job. I will manage it,' Nitin replied with a bit of anger.

'Are you from Kanpur?'

'Yes, sir,'

'From Kaushal Puri,'

'Yes, sir, but how do you know me?' Nitin asked with curiosity.

'Actually, my relatives live in that colony. Once, when I went there, I saw you that's why I was trying hard to recognise you,' the man spoke.

'OK, give me at least three to four hours. Till that time you try your best to arrange for the money,'

'Three to four hours,' Nitin said with surprise.

'I will have to manage my other officers, too. I hope you can understand,' the man winked.

'It's OK, sir. You do your job. I will wait.' Nitin stood up and came out of the office. The middle aged man got off the chair and walked towards the gallery but, instead of going inside the office, he went to a corner and started talking on his mobile.

'Hello *jijaji* (brother-in-law), how are you?'

'Yes, Rakesh, I am fine. What's going on?'

'Nothing *jijaji,* as usual,'

'Is there any special matter?'

'Do you remember Kanpur and the locality of…?' he stopped before saying the last word.

'I will not forget them even after my death,' Narendra Gupta said.

'Actually, Seetaram's son is sitting in my office,'

'For what purpose is he there?'

'Actually, there is some date of birth problem in his passport. He has come here to get it corrected and it's imperative to be corrected today itself,'

'Why?'

'He has been selected in India under-nineteen team for the world cup and the team will leave for Bangladesh tomorrow evening,'

'Hmmm,'

'I have told him to arrange for twenty thousand,'

'No, Rakesh. You will not solve his problem at any cost. Are you getting my point?' Gupta spoke.

'I understand *jijaji*. You need not worry about that.'

'Even this will be too less for what they did to us on the day of marriage of my son. Have you forgetten our insult?'

'Don't worry. He will never be able to go with the team India,' the middle aged man replied. The call was disconnected.

'Hello, sir, how are you?' After almost three hours, Nitin disturbed Rakesh Srivastava, who was extremely busy writing something on papers.

'Oh! You have come,' he stopped writing and peeped through his glasses.

'Is my problem solved? Nitin asked.

In reply, he pointed out to Nitin to sit in a chair.

'My son, I am extremely sorry. Your problem will not be solved,' he replied while chewing beetel.

'But, sir, I have arranged for twenty thousand rupees. If you ask for more, I will try to arrange more money that as well,' Nitin emphasised on his words.

'I can understand your agitation as it's a matter of your career. But my boss told me that this will take time as it is a long process and can't be done in one day.'

'But, sir,' tears started rolling down on Nitin's cheeks.

'I am sorry, my son. I can't do anything for you,' Rakesh Srivastava stood up from the chair and rubbed Nitin's shoulder for a while.

'OK, sir, thanks.' After two minutes, Nitin folded his hands to him and left the office. After reaching the bus depot, he sat in the bus and left for Kanpur. In the entire journey, tears kept rolling down on his cheeks at regular intervals by remembering the talks he used to do with his mother, Shalu and the dream he used to see of representing India under-nineteen team. A strange sadness sported his face. During the journey, he got another jolt as he got the MMS of Shalu in his message box. As he saw it, he became almost senseless. He closed his eyes and wept badly.

'Hey, why are you crying?' fellow passenger, who was sitting in a corner, as only two passengers were on a single seat, asked him. But, instead of giving him a reply, Nitin broke down even louder. This took the attention of the fellow passengers, but no one interrupted him.

FIFTY THREE

'Yes sir, what can I do?' Vinod Mathur, India under-nineteen team manager, asked the person, who entered his room along with eight guys. All were in plain dress.

'I am the S.O. of Colaba police station,' a man said by showing his identity card.

'Yes, tell me, what can I do for you?' Vinod Mathur became soft and serious.

'Sir, is there any boy named Kapil Tiwari in the India under-nineteen team,' the officer asked.

'Yes, but what is the matter?'

'One member of Under-19 team, named Kapil Tiwari has done a heinous crime and we are here to arrest him,'

'How is it possible, sir? He has been with us since yesterday and he is a very noble guy,' Vinod Mathur defended Kapil Tiwari.

'Would you like to see his innocence here itself or in front of him?' the Inspector shouted at him loudly.

'Call him, immediately,' the Inspector ordered after a pause of few seconds. Within minutes, Kapil was standing in front of everybody.

'Are you Kapil Tiwari?' the Inspector asked. Kapil nodded with fear.

'We are here to arrest you as a report has been lodged by Mr Sudhir Gupta.' As the inspector announced the name of Shalu's father's, Kapil's face turned pale and he understood the matter.

'OK, sir.' Kapil didn't oppose and started walking slowly. Vinod Mathur was still confused. He was trying to look into Kapil's eyes, but Kapil didn't give him any chance. As he was passing from the reception, he stopped and saw that his closest friend, Dinesh Tomar, was signing on the entry register. He turned up to him.

'Hey, Dinesh, you are here,' as Kapil said that, Dinesh turned back with a pale face.

'Hey, Kapil, how are you?' Dinesh said, stammering.

'You didn't give a reply,' Kapil asked.

'Actually, Kapil, I got a call from the B.C.C.I. yesterday, as I was the second standby for the World Cup,' Dinesh answered.

'Oh! Best of luck!' Kapil started walking after saying that. The police team followed him. As Kapil reached hardly fifty metres, he stopped for a while and started contemplating seriously with his eyes closed. He kept his eyes closed for almost a minute and during this he knew the foul play that his best friend, Dinesh Tomar, had played with him.

'Hey, what happened?' the S.O. asked.

'Sir, it's very urgent and an important work. I have to talk to that friend, who just came in. He is from my city,' Kapil spoke.

'OK,' the officer replied.

'Thank you very much, sir,' Kapil started pacing fast.

'Dinesh, Dinesh,' Kapil called from the back. Dinesh stopped and turned back.

'Yes, Kapil, what happened?' Dinesh asked again, stammering. But Kapil didn't respond. He first spat on Dinesh's face and then gave him a slap with full power.

'Bastard,' Kapil said loudly.

'Hey, why are you doing all this?' the S.O. intervened and dragged Kapil by holding his hand tightly.

FIFTY FOUR

'Hey, stop for a while,' Nitin pushed the rickshaw-puller from back as he noticed that a huge crowd had gathered in front of Shalu's house.

'Hey, uncle, what happened?' Nitin stopped a person and asked the question with great fear and bit of shiver.

'What I know is that a young girl has committed suicide in this house. I saw people were crying over there,' as that man replied, Nitin's face started sweating badly and became almost senseless.

'In which house, uncle?'

'In that yellow bungalow.' That person left the place after pointing out to the building.

'OK, thanks.' Nitin became weepy.

'What happened, sir? Please sit on the rickshaw. I can't wait anymore,' the rickshaw puller said.

'Brother, take your rickshaw from the back side,' Nitin said sitting in the rickshaw.

'But, that route will take a long time to reach your place.'

'Yes, I just remembered a necessary work. I will compensate. You need not worry about it,' Nitin spoke.

'No problem, if you are ready to pay,' the rickshaw-puller pulled his rickshaw back and took another route.

'Hey Nitin, you are here!' Reena spoke with surprise as she opened the gate. Nitin didn't give any response and started weeping loudly.

'Hey, Nitin, what happened, my brother. Come in.' Nitin was sobbing badly. Reena took the box of clothes from his hand.

'Tell me, what is the matter? You should be in Mumbai at this moment as your flight is due for Bangladesh in two hours.' Reena spoke.

Nitin didn't say anything. He stopped near the bed and fell on it as if a tree was cut off the roots. He kept crying out loudly for almost two minutes. Once he stopped crying, he narrated the entire story to Reena. After hearing that, Reena also broke down.

'Where is *mummy*?' Nitin asked.

'She has gone to…' Reena stopped while speaking because Savitri had gone to Shalu's house. Reena thought that Nitin didn't know about that and it would not be appropriate to tell him when he was already upset.

'She has gone to Vishal's house. I will just call her,' Reena rushed outside.

'Nitin….Nitin,' After fifteen minutes, Reena and Savitri were beating the door badly as it was closed from inside the room. It had been more than ten minutes that both the ladies were crying and beating the door.

'What happened, Savitri aunty?' Nitin's cousin, Ankit asked. He came over there listening to the noise and moaning.

'Nitin is locked inside, Ankit. He is not opening the door,' Savitri said.

What! Nitin is inside. What are you saying? He should have been in Mumbai at this moment,' Ankit spoke.

'No, he just came back half an hour back. Please do something, Ankit,' Reena said weeping. After listening to that, Ankit became nervous.

'Wait, aunty. I'll call other people.' Ankit ran outside. After ten minutes, Nitin's house was filled with almost twenty to twenty five people. All were busy breaking the door. When the door was broken, everyone entered the room. The moaning and crying became many times louder. Nitin lay down on bed and, light blue foam was coming out of his mouth. A hand written page was lying near him.

'What is this?' Vishal picked up that page.

'Leave it, Vishal. Take your friend to the hospital first,' Savitri said weeping. Everyone came into action. Soon, a car was arranged and Nitin was taken to the hospital.

FIFTY FIVE

'Hmmmm,' Jatin released his breath as Nitin finished the story. Jatin asked for a glass of water. Savitri immediately brought water for him as he gesticulated to her.

'Nitin, I think you are not my fan,' Tendulkar looked into his eyes.

'No, sir. I am a huge and the biggest fan of yours,' Nitin replied.

'Had you been my fan, you wouldn't have taken such an extreme step.' Nitin's lips were sewed as Jatin said this. He couldn't reply.

'Come what may, no one should take such an extreme step,' Jatin spoke.

'Sir, I was completely broken. My dreams, playing under-nineteen World Cup, spending life with Shalu, everything was shattered. I was surrounded by darkness,' Nitin said.

'You didn't think for a while about your parents and sister,' Jatin asked.

Tears rolled down Nitin's cheek instead of a reply.

'My advice to you, and all the youngsters, is that don't follow any celebrity like mad. Every individual has his/her own talent. If you chase any celebrity blindly, you will lose your own talent also,' Jatin said. Nitin was listening to him carefully.

'Be yourself and groom yourself. By following only this process, you can justify your talent. Yes, you can inspire and learn from others but, it's entirely impossible or madness if anyone thinks that he can become Amitabh Bachchan or Lata Mangeshkar. So, be yourself, improve your personality and establish your own identity,' Jatin said by looking into Nitin's eyes.

'You are absolutely right, sir,' Nitin spoke.

'Under-nineteen World Cup is not the end of the world. Keep your hard work going on and you will get everything, a good girlfriend as well.' Nitin gave a smile in response to Jatin's smile.

'That's great. You look so nice when you smile. Give me permission. I should make a move now.' Jatin stood up.

'Thank you so much, sir.' Nitin tried to get down from the bed.

'No, you must take rest properly,' Jatin stopped him.

Jatin called his manager and pointed out. The manager gave him a cheque book immediately.

'This is a small gift for Nitin from my side,' Jatin said that while handing over a cheque of ten lakh rupees to Nitin's mother.

'Sir, why did you give such a huge amount?' Savitri asked with modesty.

'Come on, it's very small,' Jatin said while folding his hands before her.

'OK, Nitin, bye-bye,' Nitin waved his hand.

'Sir, I want to hug you once more,' Nitin spoke.

'Jatin walked up to him and Nitin embraced him tightly.

'Thank you very much,' Nitin spoke with tears in his eyes.

'OK, Nitin, let me go now,' saying that, Jatin walked out of the room.

'Be your own self, Nitin, be your own self,' At the gate of the room, Jatin suddenly looked back and gave thumbs up to Nitin. Nitin also gave him the same response. Jatin left the room. As he came out of the hospital, the media persons surrounded his car again. Jatin came out of the car and gave a reply to them as per his promise. Having pacified the media, he sat in his car and took the route to his hotel.

FIFTY SIX

Four years later.

There was an electrifying atmosphere in the Wankhede stadium, Mumbai. The whole stadium was jam packed. Everyone was very excited and waiting for the match to start. There was restlessness and rush in the Maratha Indians dressing room. Just outside the dressing room, an emergency meeting continued of senior players and the management. As the meeting was over, Jatin Tendulkar rushed into the dressing room.

'Hey, Nitin, how are you? Why are you so sad?' Jatin said looking at Nitin. Nitin was reading the newspaper.

'Sir, today is my sister's marriage and, I am here,' Nitin replied.

'Oh! Don't worry. Be happy, there is good news for you,' Jatin spoke.

'What, sir?' Nitin asked with little sadness.

'You are going to play today's match. You are in eleven,' Jatin spoke.

'What! But, sir......' Nitin's mouth remained wide open with surprise.

'Actually, Rohit's thigh muscle got pulled while running in the warm-up session. Don't think too much and get ready within ten minutes. Take two rounds for the warm-up as well,' Jatin said. Suddenly, Jatin's eyes noticed something on Nitin's T-shirt.

'What's this? "Srivastava Poultry"' Jatin spoke while reading closely.

'Yes sir, the egg business which I started many years before has got a turn over of twenty lakh rupees per year and we have established a compand now,' Nitin said.

'That's really great. I noticed this for the first time. By the way, get ready,' Jatin spoke.

'OK, sir. I have to ask you something,' Nitin said.

'Yes,'

'Sir, I want to call up my mom as today is my debut,' Nitin spoke with innocence.

'It's not possible, Nitin. You know that using a mobile is not allowed inside the dressing room. I could have tried elsewhere, but the time is too less. The match has to be started in half an hour,' Jatin spoke

'It's OK. I was just requesting you,' Nitin said.

'Be happy and just keep your focus on the game, OK,' Jatin stressed.

'OK, sir, and thank you very much for believing in me,' Nitin said.

'Put your kit on, as early as possible,' Jatin rubbed his hand on his head with affection and came out of the dressing room.

* * *

'There is no need to be nervous. You have to focus on rotating the strike,' Jatin was giving instructions to Nitin as he entered the ground hardly one minute back. Nitin was on strike and Maratha Indians still needed twelve runs off four balls, to win the match.

'OK, sir.' Both parted to be at their respective ends.

'Oh come on, Nitin, don't worry,' Jatin spoke loudly as a beautiful late cutter completely beat him up and went into wicket-keeper's gloves. Now, three balls were left and the required runs were still twelve on the board. Super kings' foreign bowler started to run towards the bowling crease.

'Oh shit,' Jatin ran towards Nitin as the sharp rising short pitch delivery hit on Nitin's helmet, and it hit so hard that the helmet fell down on the pitch. Jatin's worry became almost double as only two balls were left and he had no other option except seeing Nitin play the next delivery, too. Players, who sat in the dug out, seemed anxious as it was a very crucial match for them.

'Are you OK, Nitin?' Jatin said after reaching close to him.

'Yes, sir. I am absolutely fine.

'Don't go by his pace and height,' Jatin said.

'Not at all, sir. It happened because of a sudden rise,' Nitin replied, wearing the helmet again. Within a minute, Nitin was on strike again. Two balls and twelve runs. The bowler started to run again. As the bowler delivered, the whole stadium echoed with loud voices and sounds.

'Well done my tiger and be cool,' Jatin said while clapping with the bat. Last ball to be delivered and six runs required. Super kings' bowler having more than six feet height, had a long discussion with his captain and the fellow players. He then ran to bowl the last delivery. It was again a short pitch ball. Nitin went for a pull, but the ball hit the outer edge and went into the skybut, was not out of the thirty yard circle and the Super kings' wicket keeper took the catch while running towards short fine leg.

Nitin sat on his knees with disappointment and Jatin too started to crawl towards Nitin with a sad face. Other side, celebrations were at its best, but only to be surprised as the umpire declared it a no ball. As the umpire declared, all the players turned their faces upto him. A smile flashed on the faces of both the batsmen.

The bowler and fielders started to crawl towards their respective area once again with sad faces. The fielders started to back up his bowler with loud sound, "Come on boy"..."Come on"..."Hit the ball again on the helmet". Gifted with a good height, the bowler ran again and gave a lot of force behind his shoulder.

It was as if Nitin had already known his plan. He shuffled more than a bit outside the off stump and sent the last delivery over the square leg boundary for a huge six. Even before the ball had landed on the ground, all the players who were sitting in the dug out, ran towards Nitin. But, Nitin rushed towards Jatin and sat down to touch his feet. Some players were rubbing his head, and some were patting on his back, but he continued to bend before Jatin for a few minutes.

He had tears of joy.

Jatin got him up and hugged him for long.

Glossary

Saale	=	(slang in India)
Chootiya	=	(slang in India)
Haramipan	=	(slang in India)
Bhai	=	(Brother)
Chhotu	=	Called fondly to a Child
Bhaiya	=	(brother)
Namaste	=	(Hi, or act of greeting to someone in India)
Didi	=	(Sister)
Lala	=	(Shopkeeper)
Mummy	=	(Mom)
Parantha	=	(fried bread)
Papa	=	(father)
Beta	=	(son, or called fondly to young guy)
Jugad	=	Temporary solution
Bhaiya-dooj	=	(The festival marks the love between brothers and sisters. On this day, sisters commemorate their brothers with an auspicious tilak, or vermillion mark on their forehead. In return, brothers give gifts to their sisters)
Kaka	=	Uncle
Kappu Baba	=	Nick name
Jaimala	=	(it's custom takes place in Hindu marriage. Through this, groom and bride put the garland around each other neck and accept to each other)
Jai and Veeru	=	(Two characters of known Indian and super hit movie. They were known for their friendship)

Chorbazzar	=	second hand market
Yaar	=	friend
Ji	=	word is added just next to the name of someone to show respect for him/her
Jija-ji	=	Brother-in-law